THE
SECRET
OF
DIVINE
CIVILIZATION

'Abdu'l-Bahá

THE SECRET OF DIVINE CIVILIZATION

translated from the Persian
by
Marzieh Gail
in consultation with
Ali-Kuli Khan

BAHÁ'Í PUBLISHING TRUST
WILMETTE, ILLINOIS 60091

Library of Congress Cataloging-in-Publication Data

Abdu'l-Bahá, 1844–1921.
 [Asrar al-ghaybiyah li-asbab al-madaniyah. English]
 The secret of divine civilization / Abdu'l-Bahá ; translated from
the Persian by Marzieh Gail. — 1st pocket-sized ed.
  p. cm.
 Translation of: Asrar al-ghaybiyah li-asbab al-madaniyah.
 Includes index.
 ISBN 0-87743-219-8 (pocketsize)
 1. Bahai Faith. 2. Civilization. I. Gail, Marzieh. II. Title.
BP360.A33 1990
297'.9317'0955—dc20   90-962
                                                                CIP

Cover design by John Solarz

INTRODUCTION

Never has the spiritual character of true civilization been revealed under such extraordinary circumstances by an author so qualified as in this text by 'Abdu'l-Bahá.

Written in the year 1875, the original Persian text was lithographed in Bombay in 1882. The first English translation was published in London, 1910, and later in Chicago, 1918, under the title *Mysterious Forces of Civilization*. The present translation by Marzieh Gail, a more accurate rendering, reflects the mastery of both languages possessed by an accomplished author whose father was Persian and whose mother was American, and who has lived for years in both countries.

The name 'Abdu'l-Bahá has attained unique fame throughout the East and the West, a symbol of wisdom, nobility, heroism and complete consecration to the cause of spiritual unity and universal peace. His name is a title meaning "Servant of Bahá." (i.e., Servant of Bahá'u'lláh)

INTRODUCTION

Born in Persia on May 23, 1844, eldest son of Bahá'u'lláh, 'Abdu'l-Bahá saw the light on the very day that 'Ali-Muḥammad, now known as the Báb, announced His mission of inaugurating a new religious Dispensation and preparing the way for Bahá'u'lláh, Author of the Bahá'í Revelation.

'Abdu'l-Bahá was but six years old when the Báb was martyred in Tabríz, eight years of age when Bahá'u'lláh was imprisoned in a dungeon in Ṭihrán by order of the Sháh, and a few months later accompanied Bahá'u'lláh on His exile to Baghdád. This commenced a period of exile and imprisonment endured by 'Abdu'l-Bahá until the year 1908. From Baghdád Bahá'u'-lláh, His family and attendants, were conducted to Constantinople, from Constantinople to Adrianople, and from Adrianople to the fortress prison in 'Akká in the Holy Land, where Bahá'u'lláh ascended in 1892. Throughout this period 'Abdu'l-Bahá, steeled in adversity, triumphant in spirit, increasingly manifested those qualities and powers upon which Bahá'u'lláh established the future of His World Faith by appointing 'Abdu'l-Bahá in His Testament the Exemplar of the religious life, the Interpreter of His Word and the Center of His Covenant with mankind.

From 1892 until 1908, 'Abdu'l-Bahá suffered extreme oppression, freed at last by the revolution in Turkey which released all political prisoners sentenced by the Sulṭán.

INTRODUCTION

It was General Allenby, military conqueror of Palestine in the first World War, who, under instructions from Lord Balfour, British Foreign Secretary, took measures to assure His protection.

From 1911 to 1913 'Abdu'l-Bahá journeyed through Europe and North America, visiting the local Bahá'í communities, addressing public audiences in peace societies, universities, churches, Negro conferences and synagogues, meeting distinguished personages in government, clerical and educational life and promulgating by example and eloquent speech the principles of universal peace. The roster of these distinguished persons is too extensive to include here, but the character of 'Abdu'l-Bahá's reception in the West may be indicated by naming, among many others, Archdeacon Wilberforce, Reverend R. J. Campbell, Lord Lamington, Sir Michael Sadler, the Maharajahs of Jalawar and Rajputana, Professor E. G. Browne, and Professor Patrick Geddes, in London; the Persian Minister, the Turkish Ambassador, "Church dignitaries of various branches of the Christian Tree," in Paris; Professor Arminius Vambery, several members of Parliament, Count Albert Apponyi, Prelate Alexander Giesswein and Professor Ignatius Goldziher, in Vienna; and in America, Dr. David Starr Jordan, Rabbi Stephen Wise, Alexander Graham Bell, Hon. Franklin K. Lane, Mrs. William Jennings Bryan, Andrew Carnegie, Hon. Franklin MacVeagh, Admiral Peary, Rabindranath Tagore.

INTRODUCTION

The recorded talks and the writings of 'Abdu'l-Bahá which seem to preserve the essence of His message to the West include the addresses delivered in City Temple, London, at Stanford University, California, in Temple Emmanuel, San Francisco, His letter addressed to the Committee on Durable Peace, The Hague, and His letter addressed to the late Dr. Forel, scientist of Switzerland. In many public talks in the United States He called upon America to lead the nations to peace, justice and social order.

In *Some Answered Questions*, Laura Barney accurately recorded 'Abdu'l-Bahá's answers to questions related to the Prophets, to man's destiny, his attributes and powers, to immortality and the life hereafter, which have long been cherished as an ideal introduction to this new age of universal religion.

The mission so faithfully fulfilled by 'Abdu'l-Bahá from 1892 to 1921 as Head of the Bahá'í World Community, providential as it was, does not directly concern the text presented in this volume.

The Secret of Divine Civilization consists of a message addressed to the rulers and the people of Persia.

. . .

The Western reader will not fail to note that 'Abdu'l-Bahá employed passages from the Qur'án on which to establish the spiritual significances of His theme and to press His appeal to the Islamic nation of Persia. Since the Qur'án is little known in the West, these passages have an incidental importance in making the Western reader more familiar with the Holy Book of the Arabic and Persian peoples at a time when understanding of the Orient is direly needed in Europe and America.

HORACE HOLLEY

July 4, 1956

THE SECRET OF DIVINE CIVILIZATION

In the Name of God the Clement, the Merciful

раise and thanksgiving be unto Providence that out of all the realities in existence He has chosen the reality of man and has honored it with intellect and wisdom, the two most luminous lights in either world. Through the agency of this great endowment, He has in every epoch cast on the mirror of creation new and wonderful configurations. If we look objectively upon the world of being, it will become apparent that from age to age, the temple of existence has continually been embellished with a fresh grace, and distinguished with an ever-varying splendor, deriving from wisdom and the power of thought.

This supreme emblem of God stands first in the order of creation and first in rank, taking precedence over all created things. Witness to it is the Holy Tradition, "Before all else, God created the mind." From the dawn of creation, it was made to be revealed in the temple of man.

Sanctified is the Lord, Who with the dazzling rays of this strange, heavenly power has made our world of darkness the envy of the worlds of light: "And the earth shall shine with the light of her Lord." [1] Holy and exalted is He, Who has caused the nature of man to be the dayspring of this boundless grace: "The God of mercy hath taught the Qur'án, hath created man, hath taught him articulate speech." [2]

O ye that have minds to know! Raise up your suppliant hands to the heaven of the one God, and humble yourselves and be lowly before Him, and thank Him for this supreme endowment, and implore Him to succor us until, in this present age, godlike impulses may radiate from the conscience of mankind, and this divinely kindled fire which has been entrusted to the human heart may never die away.

Consider carefully: all these highly varied phenomena, these concepts, this knowledge, these technical procedures and philosophical systems, these sciences, arts, industries and inventions—all are emanations of the human mind. Whatever people has ventured deeper into this shoreless sea, has come to excel the rest. The happiness and pride of a nation consist in this, that it should shine out like the sun in the high heaven of knowledge. "Shall they who have knowledge and they who have it not, be treated alike?" [3] And the honor and distinction of the individual consist in this, that he among all the world's multitudes should become a source of social good. Is any larger bounty

[1] Qur'án 39:69.
[2] Qur'án 55:1-3.
[3] Qur'án 39:12.

conceivable than this, that an individual, looking within himself, should find that by the confirming grace of God he has become the cause of peace and well-being, of happiness and advantage to his fellow men? No, by the one true God, there is no greater bliss, no more complete delight.

How long shall we drift on the wings of passion and vain desire; how long shall we spend our days like barbarians in the depths of ignorance and abomination? God has given us eyes, that we may look about us at the world, and lay hold of whatsoever will further civilization and the arts of living. He has given us ears, that we may hear and profit by the wisdom of scholars and philosophers and arise to promote and practice it. Senses and faculties have been bestowed upon us, to be devoted to the service of the general good; so that we, distinguished above all other forms of life for perceptiveness and reason, should labor at all times and along all lines, whether the occasion be great or small, ordinary or extraordinary, until all mankind are safely gathered into the impregnable stronghold of knowledge. We should continually be establishing new bases for human happiness and creating and promoting new instrumentalities toward

3

this end. How excellent, how honorable is man if he arises to fulfil his responsibilities; how wretched and contemptible, if he shuts his eyes to the welfare of society and wastes his precious life in pursuing his own selfish interests and personal advantages. Supreme happiness is man's, and he beholds the signs of God in the world and in the human soul, if he urges on the steed of high endeavor in the arena of civilization and justice. "We will surely show them Our signs in the world and within themselves." [4]

And this is man's uttermost wretchedness: that he should live inert, apathetic, dull, involved only with his own base appetites. When he is thus, he has his being in the deepest ignorance and savagery, sinking lower than the brute beasts. "They are like the brutes: Yea, they go more astray . . . For the vilest beasts in God's sight, are the deaf, the dumb, who understand not." [5]

We must now highly resolve to arise and lay hold of all those instrumentalities that promote the peace and well-being and happiness, the knowledge, culture and industry, the dignity, value and station, of the entire human race. Thus, through the restoring waters of pure intention and unselfish effort, the earth of human potentialities will blossom with its own latent excellence and flower into praiseworthy qualities, and bear and flourish until it comes to rival that rosegarden of knowledge which belonged to our forefathers. Then will this

[4] Qur'án 41:53.
[5] Qur'án 7:178; 8:22.

4

holy land of Persia become in every sense the focal center of human perfections, reflecting as if in a mirror the full panoply of world civilization.

All praise and honor be to the Dayspring of Divine wisdom, the Dawning Point of Revelation (Muḥammad), and to the holy line of His descendants, since, by the widespread rays of His consummate wisdom, His universal knowledge, those savage denizens of Yathrib (Medina) and Baṭḥá (Mecca), miraculously, and in so brief a time, were drawn out of the depths of their ignorance, rose up to the pinnacles of learning, and became centers of arts and sciences and human perfections, and stars of felicity and true civilization, shining across the horizons of the world.

His Majesty the Sháh has, at the present time, [1875] resolved to bring about the advancement of the Persian people, their welfare and security and the prosperity of their country. He has spontaneously extended assistance to his subjects, displaying energy and fair-mindedness, hoping that by the light of justice he might make Írán the envy of East and West, and set that fine fervor which characterized the first great epochs of Persia to flowing again through the veins of her people. As is clear to the discerning, the writer has for this reason felt it necessary to put down, for the sake of God alone and as a tribute to this high endeavor, a brief statement on certain urgent questions. To demonstrate that His one purpose is to promote the general welfare, He has withheld His name.[5b] Since He believes that guidance toward righteousness is in itself a righteous act, He offers these few words of counsel to His country's sons, words spoken for God's sake alone and in the spirit of a faithful friend. Our Lord, Who knows all things, bears witness that this Servant seeks nothing but what is right and good; for He, a wanderer in the desert of God's love, has come into a realm where the hand of denial or assent, of praise or blame, can touch Him not. "We nourish your souls for the sake of God; We seek from you neither recompense nor thanks." [6]

"The hand is veiled, yet the pen writes as bidden;
The horse leaps forward, yet the rider's hidden."

O people of Persia! Look into those blossoming pages that tell of another day, a time long past. Read them and wonder; see the great sight. Írán in that day was as the heart of the world; she was the bright torch flaming in the assemblage of mankind. Her power and glory shone out like the morning above the world's horizons,

---

[5b] The original Persian text written in 1875 carried no author's name, and the first English translation published in 1910 under the title *The Mysterious Forces of Civilization* states only "Written in Persian by an Eminent Bahai Philosopher."

[6] Qur'án 76:9.

and the splendor of her learning cast its rays over East and West. Word of the widespread empire of those who wore her crown reached even to the dwellers in the arctic circle, and the fame of the awesome presence of her King of Kings humbled the rulers of Greece and Rome. The greatest of the world's philosophers marveled at the wisdom of her government, and her political system became the model for all the kings of the four continents then known. She was distinguished among all peoples for the scope of her dominion, she was honored by all for her praiseworthy culture and civilization. She was as the pivot of the world, she was the source and center of sciences and arts, the wellspring of great inventions and discoveries, the rich mine of human virtues and perfections. The intellect, the wisdom of the individual members of this excellent nation dazzled the minds of other peoples, the brilliance and perceptive genius that characterized all this noble race aroused the envy of the whole world.

Aside from that which is a matter of record in Persian histories, it is stated in the Old Testament—established today, among all European peoples, as a sacred and canonical Text—that in the time of Cyrus, called in Iranian works Bahman son of Isfandíyár, the three hundred and sixty divisions of the Persian Empire extended from the inner confines of India and China to the farthermost reaches of Yemen and Ethiopia.[7] The

---

[7] 2 Chronicles 36:22-23; Ezra 1:2; Esther 1:1; 8:9; Isaiah 45:1, 14; 49:12.

Greek accounts, as well, relate how this proud sovereign came against them with an innumerable host, and left their own till then victorious dominion level with the dust. He made the pillars of all the governments to quake; according to that authoritative Arab work, the history of Abu'l-Fidá, he took over the entire known world. It is likewise recorded in this same text and elsewhere, that Firaydún, a king of the Píshdádíyán Dynasty—who was indeed, for his inherent perfections, his powers of judgment, the scope of his knowledge, and his long series of continual victories, unique among all the rulers who preceded and followed him—divided the whole known world among his three sons.

As attested by the annals of the world's most illustrious peoples, the first government to be established on earth, the foremost empire to be organized among the nations, was Persia's throne and diadem.

O people of Persia! Awake from your drunken sleep! Rise up from your lethargy! Be fair in your judgment: will the dictates of honor permit this holy land, once the wellspring of world civilization, the source of glory and joy for all mankind, the envy of East and West, to remain an object of pity, deplored by all nations? She was once the noblest of peoples: will you let contemporary history register for the ages her now degenerate state? Will you complacently accept her present wretchedness, when she was once the land of all mankind's desire? Must she now, for this contemptible sloth, this failure to struggle, this utter ignorance, be accounted the most backward of nations?

Were not the people of Persia, in days long gone, the head and front of intellect and wisdom? Did they not, by God's grace, shine out like the daystar from the horizons of Divine knowledge? How is it that we are satisfied today with this miserable condition, are engrossed in our licentious passions, have blinded ourselves to supreme happiness, to that which is pleasing in God's sight, and have all become absorbed in our selfish concerns and the search for ignoble, personal advantage?

This fairest of lands was once a lamp, streaming with the rays of Divine knowledge, of science and art, of nobility and high achievement, of wisdom and valor. Today, because of the idleness and lethargy of her people, their torpor, their undisciplined way of life, their lack of pride, lack of ambition—her bright fortune has been totally eclipsed, her light has turned to darkness. "The seven heavens and the seven earths weep over the mighty when he is brought low."

It should not be imagined that the people of Persia are inherently deficient in intelligence, or that for essential perceptiveness and understanding, inborn sagacity, intuition and wisdom, or innate capacity, they are inferior to others. God forbid! On the contrary, they have always excelled all other peoples in endowments conferred by birth. Persia herself, moreover, from the standpoint of her temperate climate and natural beauties, her geographical advantages and her rich soil, is blessed to a supreme degree. What she urgently requires, however, is deep reflection, resolute action, training, inspiration and encouragement. Her people must make a massive effort, and their pride must be aroused.

Today throughout the five continents of the globe it is Europe and most sections of America that are renowned for law and order, government and commerce, art and industry, science, philosophy and education. Yet in ancient times these were the most savage of the world's peoples, the most ignorant and brutish. They were even stigmatized as barbarians—that is, utterly rude and uncivilized. Further, from the fifth century after Christ until the fifteenth, that period defined as the Middle Ages, such terrible struggles and fierce upheavals, such ruthless encounters and horrifying acts, were the rule among the peoples of Europe, that the Europeans rightly describe those ten centuries as the Dark Ages. The basis of Europe's progress and civilization was actually laid in the fifteenth century of the Christian era, and from that time on, all her present evident culture has been, under the stimulus of great minds and as a result of the expansion of the frontiers of knowledge and the exertion of energetic and ambitious efforts, in the process of development.

Today by the grace of God and the spiritual influence of His universal Manifestation, the fair-minded ruler of Írán has gathered his people into the shelter of justice, and the sincerity of the imperial purpose has shown itself in kingly acts. Hoping that his reign will rival the glorious past, he has sought to establish equity and righteousness and to foster education and the processes of civilization throughout this noble land, and to translate from potentiality into actuality whatever will insure its progress. Not until now had we seen a monarch, holding in his capable hands the reins of affairs, and on whose high resolve the welfare of all his subjects depends, exerting as it would befit him, like a benevolent father, his efforts toward the training and cultivation of his people, seeking to insure their well-being and peace of mind, and exhibiting due concern for their interests; this Servant and those like Him have therefore remained silent. Now, however, it is clear to the discerning that the Sháh has of his own accord determined to establish a just government and to secure the progress of all his subjects. His honorable intention has consequently evoked this present statement.

It is indeed strange that instead of offering thanks for this bounty, which truly derives from the grace of Almighty God, by arising as one in gratitude and enthusiasm and praying that these noble purposes will daily multiply, some, on the contrary, whose reason has been corrupted by personal motives and the clarity of whose perception has been clouded by self-interest and conceit; whose energies are devoted to the service of their passions, whose sense of pride is perverted to the

11

love of leadership, have raised the standard of opposition and waxed loud in their complaints. Up to now, they blamed the S͟háh for not, on his own initiative, working for his people's welfare and seeking to bring about their peace and well-being. Now that he has inaugurated this great design they have changed their tune. Some say that these are newfangled methods and foreign isms, quite unrelated to the present needs and the time-honored customs of Persia. Others have rallied the helpless masses, who know nothing of religion or its laws and basic principles and therefore have no power of discrimination—and tell them that these modern methods are the practices of heathen peoples, and are contrary to the venerated canons of true faith, and they add the saying, "He who imitates a people is one of them." One group insists that such reforms should go forward with great deliberation, step by step, haste being inadmissible. Another maintains that only such measures should be adopted as the Persians themselves devise, that they themselves should reform their political administration and their educational system and the state of their culture and that there is no need to borrow improvements from other nations. Every faction, in short, follows its own particular illusion.

O people of Persia! How long will you wander? How long must your confusion last? How long will it go on, this conflict of opinions, this useless antagonism, this ignorance, this refusal to think? Others are alert, and we sleep our dreamless sleep. Other nations are making every effort to improve their condition; we are trapped in our desires and self-indulgences, and at every step we stumble into a new snare.

God is Our witness that We have no ulterior motive in developing this theme. We seek neither to curry favor with any one nor to attract any one to Ourselves nor to derive any material benefit therefrom. We speak only as one earnestly desiring the good pleasure of God, for We have turned Our gaze away from the world and its peoples and have sought refuge in the sheltering care of the Lord. "No pay do I ask of you for this . . . My reward is of God alone." [8]

Those who maintain that these modern concepts apply only to other countries and are irrelevant in Írán, that they do not satisfy her requirements or suit her way of life, disregard the fact that other nations were once as we are now. Did not these new systems and procedures, these progressive enterprises, contribute to the advancement of those countries? Were the people of Europe harmed by the adoption of such measures? Or did they rather by these means reach the highest degree of material development? Is it not true that for centuries, the people of Persia have lived as we see them living today, carrying out the pattern of the past? Have any discernible benefits resulted, has any progress been made? If these things had not been tested by experience, some in whose minds the light of native intelligence is clouded, might idly question them. On

[8] Qur'án 6:90; 11:31.

13

the contrary, however, every aspect of these prerequisites to progress have in other countries been time and again put to the test, and their benefits demonstrated so plainly that even the dullest mind can grasp them.

Let us consider this justly and without bias: let us ask ourselves which one of these basic principles and sound, well-established procedures would fail to satisfy our present needs, or would be incompatible with Persia's best political interests or injurious to the general welfare of her people. Would the extension of education, the development of useful arts and sciences, the promotion of industry and technology, be harmful things? For such endeavor lifts the individual within the mass and raises him out of the depths of ignorance to the highest reaches of knowledge and human excellence. Would the setting up of just legislation, in accord with the Divine laws which guarantee the happiness of society and protect the rights of all mankind and are an impregnable proof against assault—would such laws, insuring the integrity of the members of society and their equality before the law, inhibit their prosperity and success?

Or if by using one's perceptive faculties, one can draw analogies from present circumstances and the conclusions arrived at by collective experience, and can envisage as coming realities situations now only potential, would it be unreasonable to take such present measures as would guarantee our future security? Would it seem shortsighted, improvident and unsound,

14

would it constitute a deviation from what is right and proper, if we were to strengthen our relationships with neighboring countries, enter into binding treaties with the great powers, foster friendly connections with well-disposed governments, look to the expansion of trade with the nations of East and West, develop our natural resources and increase the wealth of our people?

Would it spell perdition for our subjects if the provincial and district governors were relieved of their present absolute authority, whereby they function exactly as they please, and were instead limited to equity and truth, and if their sentences involving capital punishment, imprisonment and the like were contingent on confirmation by the Sháh and by higher courts in the capital, who would first duly investigate the case and determine the nature and seriousness of the crime, and then hand down a just decision subject to the issuance of a decree by the sovereign? If bribery and corruption, known today by the pleasant names of gifts and favors, were forever excluded, would this threaten the foundations of justice? Would it be an evidence of unsound thinking to deliver the soldiery, who are a living sacrifice to the state and the people and brave death at every turn, from their present extreme misery and indigence, and to make adequate arrangements for their sustenance, clothing and housing, and exert every effort to instruct their officers in military science, and supply them with the most advanced types of firearms and other weapons?

Should anyone object that the above-mentioned re
forms have never yet been fully effected, he should
consider the matter impartially and know that these
deficiencies have resulted from the total absence of a
unified public opinion, and the lack of zeal and resolve
and devotion in the country's leaders. It is obvious that
not until the people are educated, not until public opin
ion is rightly focused, not until government officials,
even minor ones, are free from even the least remnant
of corruption, can the country be properly administered
Not until discipline, order and good government reach
the degree where an individual, even if he should put
forth his utmost efforts to do so, would still find him
self unable to deviate by so much as a hair's breadth
from righteousness, can the desired reforms be regarded
as fully established.

Furthermore, any agency whatever, though it be the
instrument of mankind's greatest good, is capable of
misuse. Its proper use or abuse depends on the varying
degrees of enlightenment, capacity, faith, honesty, de
votion and high-mindedness of the leaders of public
opinion.

The Sháh has certainly done his part, and the execu
tion of the proposed beneficial measures is now in the
hands of persons functioning in assemblies of consul
tation. If these individuals prove to be pure and high
minded, if they remain free from the taint of corrup
tion, the confirmations of God will make them a never
failing source of bounty to mankind. He will cause to

issue from their lips and their pens what will bless the people, so that every corner of this noble country of Írán will be illumined with their justice and integrity and the rays of that light will encompass the whole earth. "Neither will this be difficult with God." [9]

Otherwise it is clear that the results will prove unacceptable. For it has been directly witnessed in certain foreign countries that following on the establishment of parliaments those bodies actually distressed and confused the people and their well-meant reforms produced maleficent results. While the setting up of parliaments, the organizing of assemblies of consultation, constitutes the very foundation and bedrock of government, there are several essential requirements which these institutions must fulfill. First, the elected members must be righteous, God-fearing, high-minded, incorruptible. Second, they must be fully cognizant, in every particular, of the laws of God, informed as to the highest principles of law, versed in the rules which govern the management of internal affairs and the conduct of foreign relations, skilled in the useful arts of civilization, and content with their lawful emoluments.

Let it not be imagined that members of this type would be impossible to find. Through the grace of God and His chosen ones, and the high endeavors of the devoted and the consecrated, every difficulty can be easily resolved, every problem however complex will prove simpler than blinking an eye.

[9] Qur'án 14:23; 35:18.

If, however, the members of these consultative assemblies are inferior, ignorant, uninformed of the laws of government and administration, unwise, of low aim, indifferent, idle, self-seeking, no benefit will accrue from the organizing of such bodies. Where, in the past, if a poor man wanted his rights he had only to offer a gift to one individual, now he would either have to renounce all hope of justice or else satisfy the entire membership.

Close investigation will show that the primary cause of oppression and injustice, of unrighteousness, irregularity and disorder, is the people's lack of religious faith and the fact that they are uneducated. When, for example, the people are genuinely religious and are literate and well-schooled, and a difficulty presents itself, they can apply to the local authorities; if they do not meet with justice and secure their rights and if they see that the conduct of the local government is incompatible with the Divine good pleasure and the king's justice, they can then take their case to higher courts and describe the deviation of the local administration from the spiritual law. Those courts can then send for the local records of the case and in this way justice will be done. At present, however, because of their inadequate schooling, most of the population lack even the vocabulary to explain what they want.

As to those persons who, here and there, are considered leaders of the people: because this is only the beginning of the new administrative process, they are not yet sufficiently advanced in their education to have experienced the delights of dispensing justice or to have tasted the exhilaration of promoting righteousness or to have drunk from the springs of a clear conscience and a sincere intent. They have not properly understood that man's supreme honor and real happiness lie in self-respect, in high resolves and noble purposes, in integrity and moral quality, in immaculacy of mind. They have, rather, imagined that their greatness consists in the accumulation, by whatever means may offer, of worldly goods.

A man should pause and reflect and be just: his Lord, out of measureless grace, has made him a human being and honored him with the words: "Verily, We created man in the goodliest of forms" [10]—and caused His mercy which rises out of the dawn of oneness to shine down upon him, until he became the wellspring of the words of God and the place where the mysteries of heaven alighted, and on the morning of creation he was covered with the rays of the qualities of perfection and the graces of holiness. How can he stain this immaculate garment with the filth of selfish desires, or exchange this everlasting honor for infamy? "Dost thou think thyself only a puny form, when the universe is folded up within thee?" [11]

Were it not our purpose to be brief and to develop our primary subject, we would here set down a sum-

[10] Qur'án 95:4.
[11] The Imám 'Alí.

19

mary of themes from the Divine world, as to the reality of man and his high station and the surpassing value and worth of the human race. Let this be, for another time.

The highest station, the supreme sphere, the noblest, most sublime position in creation, whether visible or invisible, whether alpha or omega, is that of the Prophets of God, notwithstanding the fact that for the most part they have to outward seeming been possessed of nothing but their own poverty. In the same way, ineffable glory is set apart for the Holy Ones and those who are nearest to the Threshold of God, although such as these have never for a moment concerned themselves with material gain. Then comes the station of those just kings whose fame as protectors of the people and dispensers of Divine justice has filled the world, whose name as powerful champions of the people's rights has echoed through creation. These give no thought to amassing enormous fortunes for themselves; they believe, rather, that their own wealth lies in enriching their subjects. To them, if every individual citizen has affluence and ease, the royal coffers are full. They take no pride in gold and silver, but rather in their enlightenment and their determination to achieve the universal good.

Next in rank are those eminent and honorable ministers of state and representatives, who place the will of God above their own, and whose administrative skill and wisdom in the conduct of their office raises the science of government to new heights of perfection. They shine in the learned world like lamps of knowledge; their thinking, their attitudes and their acts demonstrate their patriotism and their concern for the country's advancement. Content with a modest stipend, they consecrate their days and nights to the execution of important duties and the devising of methods to insure the progress of the people. Through the effectiveness of their wise counsel, the soundness of their judgment, they have ever caused their government to become an example to be followed by all the governments of the world. They have made their capital city a focal center of great world undertakings, they have won distinction, attaining a supreme degree of personal eminence, and reaching the loftiest heights of repute and character.

Again, there are those famed and accomplished men of learning, possessed of praiseworthy qualities and vast erudition, who lay hold on the strong handle of the fear of God and keep to the ways of salvation. In the mirror of their minds the forms of transcendent realities are reflected, and the lamp of their inner vision derives its light from the sun of universal knowledge. They are busy by night and by day with meticulous research into such sciences as are profitable to mankind, and they devote themselves to the training of students of capacity. It is certain that to their discerning taste, the proffered treasures of kings would not compare with a single drop of the waters of knowledge, and mountains of gold and silver could not outweigh the successful solution of a difficult problem. To them, the delights that lie outside their work are only toys for children, and the cumbersome load of unnecessary possessions is only good for the ignorant and base. Content, like the birds, they give thanks for a handful of seeds, and the song of their wisdom dazzles the minds of the world's most wise.

Again, there are sagacious leaders among the people and influential personalities throughout the country, who constitute the pillars of state. Their rank and station and success depend on their being the well-wishers of the people and in their seeking out such means as will improve the nation and will increase the wealth and comfort of the citizens.

Observe the case when an individual is an eminent person in his country, zealous, wise, pure-hearted, known for his innate capacity, intelligence, natural perspicacity—and is also an important member of the state: what, for such an individual, can be regarded as honor, abiding happiness, rank and station, whether in the here or the hereafter? Is it a diligent attention to truth and righteousness, is it dedication and resolve and devotion to the good pleasure of God, is it the desire to attract the favorable consideration of the ruler and to merit the approval of the people? Or would it, rather, consist in this, that for the sake of indulging in feasts and dissipations by night he should undermine his country and break the hearts of his people by day, causing his God to reject him, and his sovereign to cast him out and his people to defame him and hold him in deserved contempt? By God, the mouldering bones in the graveyard are better than such as these! Of what value are they, who have never tasted the heavenly food of truly human qualities, and never drunk of the crystalline waters of those bounties which belong to the realm of man?

It is unquestionable that the object in establishing parliaments is to bring about justice and righteousness, but everything hinges on the efforts of the elected representatives. If their intention is sincere, desirable results and unforeseen improvements will be forthcoming; if not, it is certain that the whole thing will be meaningless, the country will come to a standstill and public affairs will continuously deteriorate. "I see a thousand builders unequal to one subverter; what then of the one builder who is followed by a thousand subverters?"

The purpose of the foregoing statements is to demonstrate at least this, that the happiness and greatness, the rank and station, the pleasure and peace, of an individual have never consisted in his personal wealth, but rather in his excellent character, his high resolve, the breadth of his learning, and his ability to solve difficult problems. How well has it been said: "On my back is a garment which, were it sold for a penny, that penny would be worth far more; yet within the garment is a soul which, if you weighed it against all the souls in the world, would prove greater and nobler."

In the present writer's view it would be preferable if the election of nonpermanent members of consultative assemblies in sovereign states should be dependent on the will and choice of the people. For elected representatives will on this account be somewhat inclined to exercise justice, lest their reputation suffer and they fall into disfavor with the public.

It should not be imagined that the writer's earlier remarks constitute a denunciation of wealth or a commendation of poverty. Wealth is praiseworthy in the highest degree, if it is acquired by an individual's own efforts and the grace of God, in commerce, agriculture, art and industry, and if it be expended for philanthropic purposes. Above all, if a judicious and resourceful individual should initiate measures which would universally enrich the masses of the people, there could be no undertaking greater than this, and it would rank in the sight of God as the supreme achievement, for such a benefactor would supply the needs and insure the comfort and well-being of a great multitude. Wealth is most commendable, provided the entire population is wealthy. If, however, a few have inordinate riches while the rest are impoverished, and no fruit or benefit accrues from that wealth, then it is only a liability to its possessor. If, on the other hand, it is expended for the promotion of knowledge, the founding of elementary and other schools, the encouragement of art and industry, the training of orphans and the poor—in brief, if it is dedicated to the welfare of society—its possessor will stand out before God and man as the most excellent of all who live on earth and will be accounted as one of the people of paradise.

As to those who maintain that the inauguration of reforms and the setting up of powerful institutions would in reality be at variance with the good pleasure of God and would contravene the laws of the Divine Law-Giver and run counter to basic religious principles and to the ways of the Prophet —let them consider how this could be the case. Would such reforms contravene the religious law because they would be acquired from foreigners and would therefore cause us to be as they are, since "He who imitates a people is one of them"? In the first place these matters relate to the temporal and material apparatus of civilization, the implements of science, the adjuncts of progress in the professions and the arts, and the orderly conduct of government. They have nothing whatever to do with the problems of the spirit and the complex realities of religious doctrine. If it be objected that even where material affairs are concerned foreign importations are inadmissible, such an argument would only establish the ignorance and absurdity of its proponents. Have they forgotten the celebrated ḥadíth (Holy Tradition): "Seek after knowledge, even unto China"? It is certain that the people of China were, in the sight of God, among the most rejected of men, because they worshiped idols and were unmindful of the omniscient Lord. The Europeans are at least "Peoples of the Book," and believers in God and specifically referred to in the sacred verse, "Thou shalt certainly find those to be nearest in affection to the believers, who say, 'We are Christians.' " [12] It is therefore quite permissible and indeed more appropriate to acquire knowledge from Christian countries. How could seeking after knowledge among the heathen be acceptable to God, and seeking it among the People of the Book be repugnant to Him?

Furthermore, in the Battle of the Confederates, Abú Sufyán enlisted the aid of the Baní Kinánih, the Baní Qahtán and the Jewish Baní Qurayzih and rose up with all the tribes of the Quraysh to put out the Divine Light that flamed in the lamp of Yathrib (Medina). In those days the great winds of trials and tribulations were blowing from every direction, as it is written: "Do

[12] Qur'án 5:85.

26

men think when they say 'We believe' they shall be let alone and not be put to proof?" [13] The believers were few and the enemy attacking in force, seeking to blot out the new-risen Sun of Truth with the dust of oppression and tyranny. Then Salmán (the Persian) came into the presence of the Prophet—the Dawning-Point of revelation, the Focus of the endless splendors of grace—and he said that in Persia to protect themselves from an encroaching host they would dig a moat or trench about their lands, and that this had proved a highly efficient safeguard against surprise attacks. Did that Wellspring of universal wisdom, that Mine of divine knowledge say in reply that this was a custom current among idolatrous, fire-worshiping Magians and could therefore hardly be adopted by monotheists? Or did He rather immediately direct His followers to set about digging a trench? He even, in His Own blessed person, took hold of the tools and went to work beside them.

It is moreover a matter of record in the books of the various Islamic schools and the writings of leading divines and historians, that after the Light of the World had risen over Ḥijáz, flooding all mankind with Its brilliance, and creating through the revelation of a new divine Law, new principles and institutions, a fundamental change throughout the world—holy laws were revealed which in some cases conformed to the prac-

[13] Qur'án 29:2.

tices of the Days of Ignorance.[14] Among these, Muhammad respected the months of religious truce,[15] retained the prohibition of swine's flesh, continued the use of the lunar calendar and the names of the months and so on. There is a considerable number of such laws specifically enumerated in the texts:

"The people of the Days of Ignorance engaged in many practices which the Law of Islám later confirmed. They would not take in marriage both a mother and her daughter, and the most shameful of acts in their view was to marry two sisters. They would stigmatize a man marrying the wife of his father, derisively calling him his father's competitor. It was their custom to go on pilgrimage to the House at Mecca, where they would perform the ceremonies of visitation, putting on the pilgrim's dress, practicing the circumambulation, running between the hills, pausing at all the stopping-places, and casting the stones. It was, furthermore, their wont to intercalate one month in every three-year period, to perform ablutions after intercourse, to rinse out the mouth and snuff up water through the nostrils, to part the hair, use the tooth-stick, pare the nails and pluck the armpits. They would, likewise, cut off the right hand of a thief."

Can one, God forbid, assume that because some of

[14] Jáhilíyyih: the period of paganism in Arabia, prior to the advent of Muhammad.

[15] The pagan Arabs observed one separate and three consecutive months of truce, during which period pilgrimages were made to Mecca, and fairs, poetry contests and similar events took place.

the divine laws resemble the practices of the Days of Ignorance, the customs of a people abhorred by all nations, it follows that there is a defect in these laws? Or can one, God forbid, imagine that the Omnipotent Lord was moved to comply with the opinions of the heathen? The divine wisdom takes many forms. Would it have been impossible for Muḥammad to reveal a Law which bore no resemblance whatever to any practice current in the Days of Ignorance? Rather, the purpose of His consummate wisdom was to free the people from the chains of fanaticism which had bound them hand and foot, and to forestall those very objections which today confuse the mind and trouble the conscience of the simple and helpless.

Some, who are not sufficiently informed as to the meaning of the divine Texts and the contents of traditional and written history, will aver that these customs of the Days of Ignorance were laws which had come down from His Holiness Abraham and had been retained by the idolaters. In this connection they will cite the Qur'ánic verse: "Follow the religion of Abraham, the sound in faith." [16] Nevertheless it is a fact attested by the writings of all the Islamic schools that the months of truce, the lunar calendar, and the cutting off of the right hand as punishment for theft, formed no part of Abraham's Law. In any case, the Pentateuch is extant and available today, and contains the laws of Abraham. Let them refer to it. They will

[16] Qur'án 16:124.

29

then, of course, insist that the Torah has been tampered with, and in proof will quote the Qur'ánic verse: "They pervert the text of the Word of God." [17] It is, however, known where such distortion has occurred, and is a matter of record in critical texts and commentaries.[18] Were We to develop the subject beyond this brief reference, We would have to abandon Our present purpose.

According to some accounts, mankind has been directed to borrow various good qualities and ways from wild animals, and to learn a lesson from these. Since it is permissible to imitate virtues of dumb animals, it is certainly far more so to borrow material sciences and techniques from foreign peoples, who at least belong to the human race and are distinguished by judgment and the power of speech. And if it be contended that such praiseworthy qualities are inborn in animals, by what proof can they claim that these essential principles of civilization, this knowledge and these sciences current among other peoples, are not inborn? Is there any Creator save God? Say: Praised be God!

The most learned and accomplished divines, the most distinguished scholars, have diligently studied those branches of knowledge the root and origin of which were the Greek philosophers such as Aristotle and the rest, and have regarded the acquisition from the Greek texts of sciences such as medicine, and

[17] Qur'án 4:45; 5:16.
[18] Cf. Bahá'u'lláh, *The Kitáb-i-Íqán,* p. 86.

branches of mathematics including algebra [19] and arithmetic, as a most valuable achievement. Every one of the eminent divines both studies and teaches the science of logic, although they consider its founder to have been a Sabean. Most of them have insisted that if a scholar has thoroughly mastered a variety of sciences but is not well grounded in logic, his opinions, deductions and conclusions cannot safely be relied upon.

It has now been clearly and irrefutably shown that the importation from foreign countries of the principles and procedures of civilization, and the acquisition from them of sciences and techniques—

[19] "If by the word *algebra* we mean that branch of mathematics by which we learn how to solve the equation $x^2 + 5x = 14$, written in this way, the science begins in the 17th century. If we allow the equation to be written with other and less convenient symbols, it may be considered as beginning at least as early as the 3rd century. If we permit it to be stated in words and solved, for simple cases of positive roots, by the aid of geometric figures, the science was known to Euclid and others of the Alexandrian school as early as 300 B.C. If we permit of more or less scientific guessing in achieving a solution, algebra may be said to have been known nearly 2000 years B.C., and it had probably attracted the attention of the intellectual class much earlier . . . The name 'algebra' is quite fortuitous. When Mohammed ibn Mûsâ al-Khowârizmî . . . wrote in Baghdad (c. 825) he gave to one of his works the name *Al-jebr w'al-muqâbalah*. The title is sometimes translated as 'restoration and equation,' but the meaning was not clear even to the later Arab writers." Encyclopedia Britannica, 1952, s.v. Algebra.

31

in brief, of whatsoever will contribute to the general good—is entirely permissible. This has been done to focus public attention on a matter of such universal advantage, so that the people may arise with all their energies to further it, until, God helping them, this Sacred Land may within a brief period become the first of nations.

O you who are wise! Consider this carefully: can an ordinary gun compare with a Martini-Henry rifle or a Krupp gun? If anyone should maintain that our old-time firearms are good enough for us and that it is useless to import weapons which have been invented abroad would even a child listen to him? Or should anyone say: "We have always transported merchandise from one country to another on the backs of animals. Why do we need steam engines? Why should we try to ape other peoples?" could any intelligent person tolerate such a statement? No, by the one God! Unless he should, because of some hidden design or animosity, refuse to accept the obvious.

Foreign nations, in spite of their having achieved the greatest expertness in science, industry and the arts, do not hesitate to borrow ideas from one another. How can Persia, a country in the direst need, be allowed to lag behind, neglected, abandoned?

Those eminent divines and men of learning who walk the straight pathway and are versed in the secrets of divine wisdom and informed of the inner realities of the sacred Books; who wear in their hearts the jewel of the fear of God, and whose luminous faces shine with the lights of salvation—these are alert to the present need and they understand the requirements of modern times, and certainly devote all their energies toward encouraging the advancement of learning and civilization. "Are they equal, those who know, and those who do not know? . . . Or is the darkness equal with the light?" [20]

The spiritually learned are lamps of guidance among the nations, and stars of good fortune shining from the horizons of humankind. They are fountains of life for such as lie in the death of ignorance and unawareness, and clear springs of perfections for those who thirst and wander in the wasteland of their defects and errors. They are the dawning places of the emblems of Divine Unity and initiates in the mysteries of the glorious Qur'án. They are skilled physicians for the ailing body of the world, they are the sure antidote to the poison that has corrupted human society. It is they who are the strong citadel guarding humanity, and the impregnable sanctuary for the sorely distressed, the anxious and tormented, victims of ignorance. "Knowledge is a light which God casteth into the heart of whomsoever He willeth."

For every thing, however, God has created a sign and symbol, and established standards and tests by which it may be known. The spiritually learned must be characterized by both inward and outward perfections; they

[20] Qur'án 39:12; 13:17.

33

must possess a good character, an enlightened nature, a pure intent, as well as intellectual power, brilliance and discernment, intuition, discretion and foresight, temperance, reverence, and a heartfelt fear of God. For an unlit candle, however great in diameter and tall, is no better than a barren palm tree or a pile of dead wood.

> *"The flower-faced may sulk or play the flirt,*
> *The cruel fair may bridle and coquet;*
> *But coyness in the ugly is ill-met,*
> *And pain in a blind eye's a double hurt."* [20a]

An authoritative Tradition states: "As for him who is one of the learned: [21] he must guard himself, defend his faith, oppose his passions and obey the commandments of his Lord. It is then the duty of the people to pattern themselves after him." Since these illustrious and holy words embody all the conditions of learning, a brief commentary on their meaning is appropriate. Whoever is lacking in these divine qualifications and does not demonstrate these inescapable requirements in his own life, should not be referred to as learned and is not worthy to serve as a model for the believers.

The first of these requirements is to guard one's own self. It is obvious that this does not refer to protecting oneself from calamities and material tests, for the

[20a] Rúmí, The *Mathnaví*, I, 1906–1907.
[21] 'Ulamá', from the Arabic *'alima*, to know, may be translated learned men, scientists, religious authorities.

Prophets and saints were, each and every one, subjected to the bitterest afflictions that the world has to offer, and were targets for all the cruelties and aggressions of mankind. They sacrificed their lives for the welfare of the people, and with all their hearts they hastened to the place of their martyrdom; and with their inward and outward perfections they arrayed humanity in new garments of excellent qualities, both acquired and inborn. The primary meaning of this guarding of oneself is to acquire the attributes of spiritual and material perfection.

The first attribute of perfection is learning and the cultural attainments of the mind, and this eminent station is achieved when the individual combines in himself a thorough knowledge of those complex and transcendental realities pertaining to God, of the fundamental truths of Qur'ánic political and religious law, of the contents of the sacred Scriptures of other faiths, and of those regulations and procedures which would contribute to the progress and civilization of this distinguished country. He should in addition be informed as to the laws and principles, the customs, conditions and manners, and the material and moral virtues characterizing the statecraft of other nations, and should be well versed in all the useful branches of learning of the day, and study the historical records of bygone governments and peoples. For if a learned individual has no knowledge of the sacred Scriptures and the entire field of divine and natural science, of religious jurisprudence and the arts of government and the varied learning of the time and the great events of history, he might prove unequal to an emergency, and this is inconsistent with the necessary qualification of comprehensive knowledge.

If for example a spiritually learned Muslim is conducting a debate with a Christian and he knows nothing of the glorious melodies of the Gospel, he will, no matter how much he imparts of the Qur'án and its truths, be unable to convince the Christian, and his words will fall on deaf ears. Should, however, the Christian observe that the Muslim is better versed in the fundamentals of Christianity than the Christian priests themselves, and understands the purport of the Scriptures even better than they, he will gladly accept the Muslim's arguments, and he would indeed have no other recourse.

When the Chief of the Exile [22] came into the presence of that Luminary of divine wisdom, of salvation and certitude, the Imám Riḍá—had the Imám, that mine of knowledge, failed in the course of their interview to base his arguments on authority appropriate and familiar to the Exilarch, the latter would never have acknowledged the greatness of His Holiness.

[22] The Resh Galuta, a prince or ruler of the exiles in Babylon, to whom Jews, wherever they were, paid tribute.

The state is, moreover, based upon two potent forces, the legislative and the executive. The focal center of the executive power is the government, while that of the legislative is the learned —and if this latter great support and pillar should prove defective, how is it conceivable that the state should stand?

In view of the fact that at the present time such fully developed and comprehensively learned individuals are hard to come by, and the government and people are in dire need of order and direction, it is essential to establish a body of scholars the various groups of whose membership would each be expert in one of the aforementioned branches of knowledge. This body should with the greatest energy and vigor deliberate as to all present and future requirements, and bring about equilibrium and order.

Up to now the religious law has not been given a decisive role in our courts, because each of the 'ulamá has been handing down decrees as he saw fit, based on his arbitrary interpretation and personal opinion. For example, two men will go to law, and one of the 'ulamá will find for the plaintiff and another for the defendant. It may even happen that in one and the same case two conflicting decisions will be handed down by the same mujtahid, on the grounds that he was inspired first in one direction and then in the other. There can be no doubt that this state of affairs has confused every important issue and must jeopardize the very foundations of society. For neither the plaintiff nor the defendant ever loses hope of eventual success, and each in turn will waste his life in the attempt to secure a later verdict which would reverse the previous one. Their entire time is thus given over to litigation, with the result that their life instead of being devoted to beneficial undertakings and necessary personal affairs, is completely involved with the dispute. Indeed, these two litigants might just as well be dead, for they can serve their government and community not a particle. If, however, a definite and final verdict were forthcoming, the duly convicted party would perforce give up all hope of reopening the case, and would then be relieved on that score and would go back to looking after his own concerns and those of others.

Since the primary means for securing the peace and tranquillity of the people, and the most effective agency for the advancement of high and low alike, is this all-important matter, it is incumbent on those learned members of the great consultative assembly who are thoroughly versed in the Divine law to evolve a single, direct and definite procedure for the settlement of litigations. This instrument should then be published throughout the country by order of the king, and its provisions should be strictly adhered to. This all-important question requires the most urgent attention.

The second attribute of perfection is justice and impartiality. This means to have no regard for one's own personal benefits and selfish advantages, and to carry out the laws of God without the slightest concern for anything else. It means to see one's self as only one of the servants of God, the All-Possessing, and except for aspiring to spiritual distinction, never attempting to be singled out from the others. It means to consider the welfare of the community as one's own. It means, in brief, to regard humanity as a single individual, and one's own self as a member of that corporeal form, and to know of a certainty that if pain or injury afflicts any member of that body, it must inevitably result in suffering for all the rest.

The third requirement of perfection is to arise with complete sincerity and purity of purpose to educate the masses: to exert the utmost effort to instruct them in the various branches of learning and useful sciences, to encourage the development of modern progress, to widen the scope of commerce, industry and the arts, to further such measures as will increase the people's wealth. For the mass of the population is uninformed as to these vital agencies which would constitute an immediate remedy for society's chronic ills.

It is essential that scholars and the spiritually learned should undertake in all sincerity and purity of intent and for the sake of God alone, to counsel and exhort the masses and clarify their vision with that collyrium which is knowledge. For today the people out of the depths of their superstition, imagine that any individual who believes in God and His signs, and in the Prophets and Divine Revelations and laws, and is a devout and God-fearing person, must of necessity remain idle and spend his days in sloth, so as to be considered in the sight of God as one who has forsaken the world and its vanities, set his heart on the life to come, and isolated himself from human beings in order to draw nearer to God. Since this theme will be developed elsewhere in the present text, We shall leave it for the moment.

Other attributes of perfection are to fear God, to love God by loving His servants, to exercise mildness and forbearance and calm, to be sincere, amenable, clement and compassionate; to have resolution and courage, trustworthiness and energy, to strive and struggle, to be generous, loyal, without malice, to have zeal and a sense of honor, to be high-minded and magnanimous, and to have regard for the rights of others. Whoever is lacking in these excellent human qualities is defective. If We were to explain the inner meanings of each one of these attributes, "the poem would take up seventy maunds [22a] of paper."

[22a] A measure of weight, in Ṭihrán equivalent to six and two-thirds pounds.

The second of these spiritual standards which apply to the possessor of knowledge is that he should be the defender of his faith. It is obvious that these holy words do not refer exclusively to searching out the implications of the Law, observing the forms of worship, avoiding greater and lesser sins, practicing the religious ordinances, and by all these methods, protecting the Faith. They mean rather that the whole population should be protected in every way; that every effort should be exerted to adopt a combination of all possible measures to raise up the Word of God, increase the number of believers, promote the Faith of God and exalt it and make it victorious over other religions.

If, indeed, the Muslim religious authorities had persevered along these lines as they ought to have done, by now every nation on earth would have been gathered into the shelter of the unity of God and the bright fire of "that He may make it victorious over every other religion" [23] would have flamed out like the sun in the midmost heart of the world.

Fifteen centuries after Christ, Luther, who was originally one of the twelve members of a Catholic religious body at the center of the Papal government and later on initiated the Protestant religious belief, op-

[23] Qur'án 9:33; 48:28; 61:9.

41

posed the Pope on certain points of doctrine such as the prohibition of monastic marriage, the revering and bowing down before images of the Apostles and Christian leaders of the past, and various other religious practices and ceremonies which were accretional to the ordinances of the Gospel. Although at that period the power of the Pope was so great and he was regarded with such awe that the kings of Europe shook and trembled before him, and he held control of all Europe's major concerns in the grasp of his might—nevertheless because Luther's position as regards the freedom of religious leaders to marry, the abstention from worshiping and making prostrations before images and representations hung in the churches, and the abrogation of ceremonials which had been added on to the Gospel, was demonstrably correct, and because the proper means were adopted for the promulgation of his views: within these last four hundred and some years the majority of the population of America, four-fifths of Germany and England and a large percentage of Austrians, in sum about one hundred and twenty-five million people drawn from other Christian denominations, have entered the Protestant Church. The leaders of this religion are still making every effort to promote it, and today on the East Coast of Africa, ostensibly to emancipate the Sudanese and various Negro peoples, they have established schools and colleges and are training and civilizing completely savage African tribes, while their true and primary purpose is to convert some of the Muslim Negro tribes to Protestantism. Every community is toiling for the advancement of its people, and we (i.e., Muslims) sleep on!

Although it was not clear what purpose impelled this man or where he was tending, see how the zealous efforts of Protestant leaders have spread his doctrines far and wide.

Now if the illustrious people of the one true God, the recipients of His confirmations, the objects of His Divine assistance, should put forth all their strength, and with complete dedication, relying upon God and turning aside from all else but Him, should adopt procedures for spreading the Faith and should bend all their efforts to this end, it is certain that His Divine light would envelop the whole earth.

A few, who are unaware of the reality below the surface of events, who cannot feel the pulse of the world under their fingers, who do not know what a massive dose of truth must be administered to heal this chronic old disease of falsehood, believe that the Faith can only be spread by the sword, and bolster their opinion with the Tradition, "I am a Prophet by the sword." If, however, they would carefully examine this question, they would see that in this day and age the sword is not a suitable means for promulgating the Faith, for it would only fill peoples' hearts with revulsion and terror. According to the Divine Law of Muḥammad, it is not permissible to compel the People of the Book to acknowledge and accept the Faith. While it is a sacred obligation devolving on every conscientious believer in the unity of God to guide mankind to the truth, the Traditions "I am a Prophet by the sword" and "I am commanded to threaten the lives of the people until they say, 'There is none other God but God'" referred to the idolaters of the Days of Ignorance, who in their blindness and bestiality had sunk below the level of human beings. A faith born of sword thrusts could hardly be relied upon, and would for any trifling cause revert to error and unbelief. After the ascension of Muḥammad, and His passing to "the seat of truth, in the presence of the potent King," [24] the tribes around Medina apostatized from their Faith, turning back to the idolatry of pagan times.

Remember when the holy breaths of the Spirit of God (Jesus) were shedding their sweetness over Palestine and Galilee, over the shores of Jordan and the regions around Jerusalem, and the wondrous melodies of the Gospel were sounding in the ears of the spiritually illumined, all the peoples of Asia and Europe, of Africa and America, of Oceania, which comprises the islands and archipelagoes of the Pacific and Indian Oceans, were fire-worshipers and pagans, ignorant of the Divine Voice that spoke out on the Day of the Covenant.[25] Alone the Jews believed in the divinity and oneness of God. Following the declaration of Jesus, the pure

[24] Qur'án 54:55.

[25] Qur'án 7:171: Yawm-i-Alast, the Day when God, addressing Adam's posterity-to-be, said to them, "Am I not your Lord?" (a-lastu bi Rabbikum) and they replied: "Yea, we bear witness."

44

and reviving breath of His mouth conferred eternal life on the inhabitants of those regions for a period of three years, and through Divine Revelation the Law of Christ, at that time the vital remedy for the ailing body of the world, was established. In the days of Jesus only a few individuals turned their faces toward God; in fact only the twelve disciples and a few women truly became believers, and one of the disciples, Judas Iscariot apostatized from his Faith, leaving eleven. After the ascension of Jesus to the Realm of Glory, these few souls stood up with their spiritual qualities and with deeds that were pure and holy, and they arose by the power of God and the life-giving breaths of the Messiah to save all the peoples of the earth. Then all the idolatrous nations as well as the Jews rose up in their might to kill the Divine fire that had been lit in the lamp of Jerusalem. "Fain would they put out God's light with their mouths: but God hath willed to perfect His light, albeit the infidels abhor it." [26] Under the fiercest tortures, they did every one of these holy souls to death; with butchers' cleavers, they chopped the pure and undefiled bodies of some of them to pieces and burned them in furnaces, and they stretched some of the followers on the rack and then buried them alive. In spite of this agonizing requital, the Christians continued to teach the Cause of God, and they never drew a sword from its scabbard or even so much as grazed a cheek. Then in the end the Faith of Christ encom-

[26] Qur'án 9:33.

passed the whole earth, so that in Europe and America no traces of other religions were left, and today in Asia and Africa and Oceania, large masses of people are living within the sanctuary of the Four Gospels.

It has now by the above irrefutable proofs been fully established that the Faith of God must be propagated through human perfections, through qualities that are excellent and pleasing, and spiritual behavior. If a soul of his own accord advances toward God he will be accepted at the Threshold of Oneness, for such a one is free of personal considerations, of greed and selfish interests, and he has taken refuge within the sheltering protection of his Lord. He will become known among men as trustworthy and truthful, temperate and scrupulous, high-minded and loyal, incorruptible and God-fearing. In this way the primary purpose in revealing the Divine Law—which is to bring about happiness in the after life and civilization and the refinement of character in this—will be realized. As for the sword, it will only produce a man who is outwardly a believer, and inwardly a traitor and apostate.

We shall here relate a story that will serve as an example to all. The Arabian chronicles tell how, at a time prior to the advent of Muḥammad, Nu'mán son of Mundhir the Lakhmite

—an Arab king in the Days of Ignorance, whose seat of government was the city of Ḥírih—had one day returned so often to his wine-cup that his mind clouded over and his reason deserted him. In this drunken and insensible condition he gave orders that his two boon companions, his close and much-loved friends, Khálid son of Mudallil and 'Amr son of Mas'úd-Kaldih, should be put to death. When he wakened after his carousal, he inquired for the two friends and was given the grievous news. He was sick at heart, and because of his intense love and longing for them, he built two splendid monuments over their two graves and he named these the Smeared-With-Blood.

Then he set apart two days out of the year, in memory of the two companions, and he called one of them the Day of Evil and one the Day of Grace. Every year on these two appointed days he would issue forth with pomp and circumstance and sit between the monuments. If, on the Day of Evil, his eye fell on any soul, that person would be put to death; but on the Day of Grace, whoever passed would be overwhelmed with gifts and benefits. Such was his rule, sealed with a mighty oath and always rigidly observed.

One day the king mounted his horse, that was called Maḥmúd, and rode out into the plains to hunt. Suddenly in the distance he caught sight of a wild donkey. Nu'mán urged on his horse to overtake it, and galloped away at such speed that he was cut off from his retinue. As night approached, the king was hopelessly lost.

Then he made out a tent, far off in the desert, and he turned his horse and headed toward it. When he reached the entrance of the tent he asked, "Will you receive a guest?" The owner (who was Ḥanzala, son of Abí-Ghafráy-i-Ṭá'í) replied, "Yea." He came forward and helped Nu'mán to dismount. Then he went to his wife and told her, "There are clear signs of greatness in the bearing of this person. Do your best to show him hospitality, and make ready a feast." His wife said, "We have a ewe. Sacrifice it. And I have saved a little flour against such a day." Ḥanzala first milked the ewe and carried a bowl of milk to Nu'mán, and then he slaughtered her and prepared a meal; and what with his friendliness and loving-kindness, Nu'mán spent that night in peace and comfort. When dawn came, Nu'mán made ready to leave, and he said to Ḥanzala: "You have shown me the utmost generosity, receiving and feasting me. I am Nu'mán, son of Mundhir, and I shall eagerly await your arrival at my court."

Time passed, and famine fell on the land of Ṭayy. Ḥanzala was in dire need and for this reason he sought out the king. By a strange coincidence he arrived on the Day of Evil. Nu'mán was greatly troubled in spirit. He began to reproach his friend, saying, "Why did you come to your friend on this day of all days? For this is the Day of Evil, that is, the Day of Wrath and the Day of Distress. This day, should my eyes alight on Qábús, my only son, he should not escape with his life. Now ask me whatever favor you will."

Ḥanẓala said: "I knew nothing of your Day of Evil. As for the gifts of this life, they are meant for the living, and since I at this hour must drink of death, what can all the world's storehouses avail me now?"

Nuʿmán said, "There is no help for this."

Ḥanẓala told him: "Respite me, then, that I may go back to my wife and make my testament. Next year I shall return, on the Day of Evil."

Nuʿmán then asked for a guarantor, so that, if Ḥanẓala should break his word, this guarantor would be put to death instead. Ḥanẓala, helpless and bewildered, looked about him. Then his gaze fell on one of Nuʿmán's retinue, Sharík, son of ʿAmr, son of Qays of Shaybán, and to him he recited these lines: "O my partner, O son of ʿAmr! Is there any escape from death? O brother of every afflicted one! O brother of him who is brotherless! O brother of Nuʿmán, in thee today is a surety for the Shaykh. Where is Shaybán the noble— may the All-Merciful favor him!" But Sharík only answered, "O my brother, a man cannot gamble with his life." At this the victim could not tell where to turn. Then a man named Qarád, son of Adjaʿ the Kalbite stood up and offered himself as a surety, agreeing that, should he fail on the next Day of Wrath to deliver up the victim, the king might do with him, Qarád, as he wished. Nuʿmán then bestowed five hundred camels on Ḥanẓala, and sent him home.

In the following year on the Day of Evil, as soon as the true dawn broke in the sky, Nuʿmán as was his

custom set out with pomp and pageantry and made for
the two mausoleums called the Smeared-With-Blood.
He brought Qarád along, to wreak his kingly wrath
upon him. The pillars of the state then loosed their
tongues and begged for mercy, imploring the king to
respite Qarád until sundown, for they hoped that
Ḥanzala might yet return; but the king's purpose was
to spare the life of Ḥanzala, and to requite his hospitality by putting Qarád to death in his place. As the
sun began to set, they stripped off the garments of
Qarád, and made ready to sever his head. At that
moment a rider appeared in the distance, galloping at
top speed. Nu'mán said to the swordsman, "Why de-
layest thou?" The ministers said, "Perchance it is Ḥanzala who comes." And when the rider drew near, they
saw it was none other.

Nu'mán was sorely displeased. He said, "Thou fool!
Thou didst slip away once from the clutching fingers
of death; must thou provoke him now a second time?"

And Ḥanzala answered, "Sweet in my mouth and
pleasant on my tongue is the poison of death, at the
thought of redeeming my pledge."

Nu'mán asked, "What could be the reason for this
trustworthiness, this regard for thine obligation and this
concern for thine oath?" And Ḥanzala answered, "It
is my faith in the one God and in the Books that have
come down from heaven." Nu'mán asked, "What Faith
dost thou profess?" And Ḥanzala said, "It was the holy
breaths of Jesus that brought me to life. I follow the

straight pathway of Christ, the Spirit of God." Nu'mán said, "Let me inhale these sweet aromas of the Spirit."

So it was that Ḥanzala drew out the white hand of guidance from the bosom of the love of God,[27] and illumined the sight and the insight of the beholders with the Gospel light. After he had in bell-like accents recited some of the divine verses out of the Evangel, Nu'mán and all his ministers sickened of their idols and their idol-worship and were confirmed in the Faith of God. And they said, "Alas, a thousand times alas, that up to now we were careless of this infinite mercy and veiled away therefrom, and were bereft of this rain from the clouds of the grace of God." Then straightway the king tore down the two monuments called the Smeared-With-Blood, and he repented of his tyranny and established justice in the land.

[27] Cf. Qur'án 27:12, referring to Moses: "Put now thy hand into thy bosom: it shall come forth white . . . one of nine signs to Pharaoh and his people. . . ." Also Qur'án 7:105; 20:23; 26:32; and 28:32. Also Exodus 4:6. See too Edward Fitzgerald's *The Rubaiyat of Omar Khayyam*:

> Now the New Year reviving old Desires,
> The thoughtful Soul to Solitude retires,
> Where the White Hand of Moses on the Bough
> Puts out, and Jesus from the Ground suspires.

The metaphors here refer to white blossoms and the perfumes of spring.

Observe how one individual, and he a man of the desert, to outward seeming unknown and of no station—because he showed forth one of the qualities of the pure in heart, was able to deliver this proud sovereign and a great company of others from the dark night of unbelief and guide them into the morning of salvation; to save them from the perdition of idolatry and bring them to the shores of the oneness of God, and to put an end to practices of the sort which blight a whole society and reduce the peoples to barbarism. One must think deeply over this, and grasp its meaning.

My heart aches, for I note with intense regret that the attention of the people is nowhere directed toward that which is worthy of this day and time. The Sun of Truth has risen above the world but we are ensnared in the dark of our imaginings. The waters of the Most Great Sea are surging all around us, while we are parched and weak with thirst. The divine bread is coming down from heaven, and yet we grope and stumble in a famine-stricken land. "Between the weeping and the telling, I spin out my days."

One of the principal reasons why people of other religions have shunned and failed to become converted to the Faith of God is fanaticism and unreasoning religious zeal. See for example the divine words that were addressed to Muḥammad, the Ark of Salvation, the Luminous Countenance and Lord of Men, bidding Him to be gentle with the people and long-suffering: "Debate with them in the kindliest manner." [28] That Blessed Tree Whose light was "neither of the East nor of the West" [29] and Who cast over all the peoples of the earth the sheltering shade of a measureless grace, showed forth infinite kindness and forbearance in His dealings with every one. In these words, likewise, were Moses and Aaron commanded to challenge Pharaoh, Lord of the Stakes: [30] "Speak ye to him with gentle speech." [31]

Although the noble conduct of the Prophets and Holy Ones of God is widely known, and it is indeed, until the coming of the Hour,[32] in every aspect of life

[28] Qur'án 16:126.

[29] Qur'án 24:35.

[30] Dhu'l-Awtád is variously rendered by translators of the Qur'án as The Impaler, The Contriver of the Stakes, The Lord of a Strong Dominion, The One Surrounded by Ministers, etc. Awtád means pegs or tent stakes. See Qur'án 38:11 and 89:9.

[31] Qur'án 20:46.

[32] Qur'án 33:63: "Men will ask Thee of 'the Hour.' Say: The knowledge of it is with God alone." Cf. also 22:1, "the earth-

an excellent pattern for all mankind to follow, nevertheless some have remained neglectful of and separated from these qualities of extraordinary sympathy and loving-kindness, and have been prevented from attaining to the inner significances of the Holy Books. Not only do they scrupulously shun the adherents of religions other than their own, they do not even permit themselves to show them common courtesy. If one is not allowed to associate with another, how can one guide him out of the dark and empty night of denial, of "there-is-no-God," into the bright morning of belief, and the affirmation, "but God." [33] And how can one urge him on and encourage him to rise up out of the abyss of perdition and ignorance and climb the heights of salvation and knowledge? Consider justly: had not Ḥanzala treated Nu'mán with true friendship, showing him kindness and hospitality, could he have brought the King and a great number of other idolaters to acknowledge the unity of God? To keep aloof from people, to shun them, to be harsh with them, will make them shrink away, while affection and consideration, mildness and forbearance will attract their hearts toward God. If a true believer when meeting an individual from a foreign country should express revulsion, and

quake of the Hour," etc. See also Matthew 24:36, 42, etc. To Bahá'ís, this refers to the Advent of the Báb and Bahá'u'lláh.

[33] Cf. the Islamic confession of faith, sometimes called the two testimonies: "I testify that there is no God but God and Muḥammad is the Prophet of God."

should speak the horrible words forbidding association with foreigners and referring to them as "unclean," the stranger would be grieved and offended to such a point that he would never accept the Faith, even if he should see, taking place before his very eyes, the miracle of the splitting of the moon. The results of shunning him would be this, that if there had been in his heart some faint inclination toward God, he would repent of it, and would flee away from the sea of faith into the wastes of oblivion and unbelief. And upon returning home to his own country he would publish in the press statements to the effect that such and such a nation was utterly lacking in the qualifications of a civilized people.

If we ponder a while over the Qur'ánic verses and proofs, and the traditional accounts which have come down to us from those stars of the heaven of Divine Unity, the Holy Imáms, we shall be convinced of the fact that if a soul is endowed with the attributes of true faith and characterized with spiritual qualities he will become to all mankind an emblem of the outstretched mercies of God. For the attributes of the people of faith are justice and fair-mindedness; forbearance and compassion and generosity; consideration for others; candor, trustworthiness, and loyalty; love and loving-kindness; devotion and determination and humanity. If therefore an individual is truly righteous, he will avail himself of all those means which will attract the hearts of men, and through the attributes of God he will draw them to the straight path of faith and cause them to drink from the river of everlasting life.

Today we have closed our eyes to every righteous act and have sacrificed the abiding happiness of society to our own transitory profit. We regard fanaticism and zealotry as redounding to our credit and honor, and not content with this, we denounce one another and plot each other's ruin, and whenever we wish to put on a show of wisdom and learning, of virtue and godliness, we set about mocking and reviling this one and that. "The ideas of such a one," we say, "are wide of the mark, and so-and-so's behavior leaves much to be desired. The religious observances of Zayd are few and far between, and 'Amr is not firm in his faith. So-and-so's opinions smack of Europe. Fundamentally, Blank thinks of nothing but his own name and fame. Last night when the congregation stood up to pray, the row was out of line, and it is not permissible to follow a different leader. No rich man has died this month, and nothing has been offered to charity in memory of the Prophet. The edifice of religion has crumbled, the foundations of faiths have been blown to the winds. The carpet of belief has been rolled up, the tokens of certitude blotted out; the whole world has fallen into error; when it comes to repelling tyranny all are soft and remiss. Days and months have passed away, and these villages and estates still belong to the same owners as they did last year. In this town there used to be seventy different governments functioning in good order, but the number has steadily decreased; there are only twenty-five left now, as a memento. It used to be that two hundred contradictory judgments were handed down by the same muftí in any one day, now we hardly get fifty. In those days there were crowds of people who were all brainsick with litigation, and now they rest in peace; today the plaintiff would be defeated and the defendant victorious, tomorrow the plaintiff won the case and the defendant lost it—but now this excellent practice has been abandoned too. What is this heathenish religion, this idolatrous kind of error! Alas for the Law, alas for the Faith, alas for all these calamities! O Brothers in the Faith! This is surely the end of the world! The Judgment is coming!"

With words such as these they assault the minds of the helpless masses and disturb the hearts of the already bewildered poor, who know nothing of the true state of affairs and the real basis for all such talk, and remain completely unaware of the fact that a thousand selfish purposes are concealed behind the supposedly religious eloquence of certain individuals. They imagine that speakers of this type are motivated by virtuous zeal, when the truth is that such individuals keep up a great hue and cry because they see their own personal ruin in the welfare of the masses, and believe that if the people's eyes are opened, their own light will go out. Only the keenest insight will detect the fact that if the hearts of these individuals were really impelled by righteousness and the fear of God, the fragrance of it would, like musk, be spreading everywhere. Nothing in the world can ever be supported by words alone.

But these ill-omened owls have done a wrong,
And learned to sing as the white falcon sings.
And what of Sheba's message that the lapwing brings
If the bittern learn to sing the lapwing's song? [34]

The spiritually learned, those who have derived infinite significance and wisdom from the Book of Divine Revelation, and whose illumined hearts draw inspiration from the unseen world of God, certainly exert their efforts to bring about the supremacy of the true followers of God, in all respects and above all peoples, and they toil and struggle to make use of every agency that will conduce to progress. If any man neglects these high purposes he can never prove acceptable in the sight of God; he stands out with all his shortcomings and claims perfection, and destitute, pretends to wealth.

One sluggish, blind and surly's a poor thing,
"A lump of flesh, without a foot or wing."
How far is he who apes and makes a show
From the illumined, who doth truly know.
One but an echo, though it's clear and sharp,
And one, the Psalmist David with his harp.

Knowledge, purity, devotion, discipline, independence, have nothing to do with outer appearance and dress. Once in the course of My travels I heard an

[34] Cf. Qur'án 27:20 ff.

58

eminent personage make the following excellent re-
mark, the wit and charm of which remain in memory:
"Not every cleric's turban is a proof of continence and
knowledge; not every layman's hat a sign of ignorance
and immorality. How many a hat has proudly raised
the banner of knowledge, how many a turban pulled
down the Law of God!"

The third element of the utterance under discussion is, "opposes his passions." How wonderful are the implications of this deceptively
easy, all-inclusive phrase. This is the very foundation
of every laudable human quality; indeed, these few
words embody the light of the world, the impregnable
basis of all the spiritual attributes of human beings.
This is the balance wheel of all behavior, the means of
keeping all man's good qualities in equilibrium.

For desire is a flame that has reduced to ashes un-
counted lifetime harvests of the learned, a devouring
fire that even the vast sea of their accumulated knowledge could never quench. How often has it happened
that an individual who was graced with every attribute
of humanity and wore the jewel of true understanding,
nevertheless followed after his passions until his excellent qualities passed beyond moderation and he was
forced into excess. His pure intentions changed to evil

ones, his attributes were no longer put to uses worthy of them, and the power of his desires turned him aside from righteousness and its rewards into ways that were dangerous and dark. A good character is in the sight of God and His chosen ones and the possessors of insight, the most excellent and praiseworthy of all things, but always on condition that its center of emanation should be reason and knowledge and its base should be true moderation. Were the implications of this subject to be developed as they deserve the work would grow too long and our main theme would be lost to view.

All the peoples of Europe, notwithstanding their vaunted civilization, sink and drown in this terrifying sea of passion and desire, and this is why all the phenomena of their culture come to nothing. Let no one wonder at this statement or deplore it. The primary purpose, the basic objective, in laying down powerful laws and setting up great principles and institutions dealing with every aspect of civilization, is human happiness; and human happiness consists only in drawing closer to the Threshold of Almighty God, and in securing the peace and well-being of every individual member, high and low alike, of the human race; and the supreme agencies for accomplishing these two objectives are the excellent qualities with which humanity has been endowed.

A superficial culture, unsupported by a cultivated morality, is as "a confused medley of dreams," [35] and

[35] Qur'án 12:44; 21:5.

external lustre without inner perfection is "like a vapor in the desert which the thirsty dreameth to be water." [36] For results which would win the good pleasure of God and secure the peace and well-being of man, could never be fully achieved in a merely external civilization.

The peoples of Europe have not advanced to the higher planes of moral civilization, as their opinions and behavior clearly demonstrate. Notice, for example, how the supreme desire of European governments and peoples today is to conquer and crush one another, and how, while harboring the greatest secret repulsion, they spend their time exchanging expressions of neighborly affection, friendship and harmony.

There is the well-known case of the ruler who is fostering peace and tranquillity and at the same time devoting more energy than the warmongers to the accumulation of weapons and the building up of a larger army, on the grounds that peace and harmony can only be brought about by force. Peace is the pretext, and night and day they are all straining every nerve to pile up more weapons of war, and to pay for this their wretched people must sacrifice most of whatever they are able to earn by their sweat and toil. How many thousands have given up their work in useful industries and are laboring day and night to produce new and deadlier weapons which would spill out the blood of the race more copiously than before.

Each day they invent a new bomb or explosive and

[36] Qur'án 24:39.

then the governments must abandon their obsolete arms and begin producing the new, since the old weapons cannot hold their own against the new. For example at this writing, in the year 1292 A.H.[37] they have invented a new rifle in Germany and a bronze cannon in Austria, which have greater firepower than the Martini-Henry rifle and the Krupp cannon, are more rapid in their effects and more efficient in annihilating humankind. The staggering cost of it all must be borne by the hapless masses.

Be just: can this nominal civilization, unsupported by a genuine civilization of character, bring about the peace and well-being of the people or win the good pleasure of God? Does it not, rather, connote the destruction of man's estate and pull down the pillars of happiness and peace?

At the time of the Franco-Prussian War, in the year 1870 of the Christian era, it was reported that 600,000 men died, broken and beaten, on the field of battle. How many a home was torn out by the roots; how many a city, flourishing the night before, was toppled down by sunrise. How many a child was orphaned and abandoned, how many an old father and mother had to see their sons, the young fruit of their lives, twisting and dying in dust and blood. How many women were widowed, left without a helper or protector.

And then there were the libraries and magnificent buildings of France that went up in flames, and the

[37] 1875 A.D.

military hospital, packed with sick and wounded men, that was set on fire and burned to the ground. And there followed the terrible events of the Commune, the savage acts, the ruin and horror when opposing factions fought and killed one another in the streets of Paris. There were the hatreds and hostilities between Catholic religious leaders and the German government. There was the civil strife and uproar, the bloodshed and havoc brought on between the partisans of the Republic and the Carlists in Spain.

Only too many such instances are available to demonstrate the fact that Europe is morally uncivilized. Since the writer has no wish to cast aspersions on anyone He has confined Himself to these few examples. It is clear that no perceptive and well-informed mind can countenance such events. Is it right and proper that peoples among whom, diametrically opposed to the most desirable human behavior, such horrors take place, should dare lay claim to a real and adequate civilization? Especially when out of all this no results can be hoped for except the winning of a transient victory; and since this outcome never endures, it is, to the wise, not worth the effort.

Time and again down the centuries, the German state has subdued the French; over and over, the kingdom of France has governed German land. Is it permissible that in our day 600,000 helpless creatures should be offered up as a sacrifice to such nominal and temporary uses and results? No, by the Lord God! Even a child can see the evil of it. Yet the pursuit of passion and desire will wrap the eyes in a thousand veils that rise out of the heart to blind the sight and the insight as well.

> *Desire and self come in the door*
> *And blot out virtue, bright before,*
> *And a hundred veils will rise*
> *From the heart, to blind the eyes.*

True civilization will unfurl its banner in the midmost heart of the world whenever a certain number of its distinguished and high-minded sovereigns—the shining exemplars of devotion and determination—shall, for the good and happiness of all mankind, arise, with firm resolve and clear vision, to establish the Cause of Universal Peace. They must make the Cause of Peace the object of general consultation, and seek by every means in their power to establish a Union of the nations of the world. They must conclude a binding treaty and establish a covenant, the provisions of which shall be sound, inviolable and definite. They must proclaim it to all the world and obtain for it the sanction of all the human race. This supreme and noble undertaking—the real source of the peace and well-being of all the world—should be regarded as sacred by all that dwell on earth. All the forces of humanity must be mobilized to ensure the stability and permanence of this Most Great Covenant. In this all-embracing Pact the limits and frontiers of each and every nation should be clearly fixed, the principles underlying the relations of governments towards one another definitely laid down, and all international agreements and obligations ascertained. In like manner, the size of the armaments of every government should be strictly limited, for if the preparations for war and the military forces of any nation should be allowed to increase, they will arouse the suspicion of others. The fundamental principle underlying this solemn Pact should be so fixed that if any government later violate any one of its provisions, all the governments on earth should arise to reduce it to utter submission, nay the human race as a whole should resolve, with every power at its disposal, to destroy that government. Should this greatest of all remedies be applied to the sick body of the world, it will assuredly recover from its ills and will remain eternally safe and secure.[38]

Observe that if such a happy situation be forthcoming, no government would need continually to pile up the weapons of war, nor feel itself obliged to produce ever new military weapons with which to conquer the human race. A small force for the purposes of internal security, the correction of criminal and disorderly elements and the prevention of local disturbances, would be required—no more. In this way the entire population would, first of all, be relieved of the crushing burden

[38] The foregoing paragraph, together with the later paragraph beginning "A few, unaware of the power latent in human endeavor," was translated by Shoghi Effendi, Guardian of the Bahá'í Faith. Cf. *The World Order of Bahá'u'lláh,* pp. 37-38.

of expenditure currently imposed for military purposes, and secondly, great numbers of people would cease to devote their time to the continual devising of new weapons of destruction—those testimonials of greed and bloodthirstiness, so inconsistent with the gift of life—and would instead bend their efforts to the production of whatever will foster human existence and peace and well-being, and would become the cause of universal development and prosperity. Then every nation on earth will reign in honor, and every people will be cradled in tranquillity and content.

A few, unaware of the power latent in human endeavor, consider this matter as highly impracticable, nay even beyond the scope of man's utmost efforts. Such is not the case, however. On the contrary, thanks to the unfailing grace of God, the loving-kindness of His favored ones, the unrivaled endeavors of wise and capable souls, and the thoughts and ideas of the peerless leaders of this age, nothing whatsoever can be regarded as unattainable. Endeavor, ceaseless endeavor, is required. Nothing short of an indomitable determination can possibly achieve it. Many a cause which past ages have regarded as purely visionary, yet in this day has become most easy and practicable. Why should this most great and lofty Cause—the daystar of the firmament of true civilization and the cause of the glory, the advancement, the well-being and the success of all humanity—be regarded as impossible of achievement? Surely the day will come when its beauteous light shall shed illumination upon the assemblage of man.

The apparatus of conflict will, as preparations go on at their present rate, reach the point where war will become something intolerable to mankind.

It is clear from what has already been said that man's glory and greatness do not consist in his being avid for blood and sharp of claw, in tearing down cities and spreading havoc, in butchering armed forces and civilians. What would mean a bright future for him would be his reputation for justice, his kindness to the entire population whether high or low, his building up countries and cities, villages and districts, his making life easy, peaceful and happy for his fellow beings, his laying down fundamental principles for progress, his raising the standards and increasing the wealth of the entire population.

Consider how throughout history many a king has sat on his throne as a conqueror. Among them were Hulágú Khán and Tamerlane, who took over the vast continent of Asia, and Alexander of Macedon and Napoleon I, who stretched their arrogant fists over three of the earth's five continents. And what was gained by all their mighty victories? Was any country made to flourish, did any happiness result, did any throne stand? Or was it rather that those reigning houses lost their power? Except that Asia went up in the flame of many battles and fell away to ashes, Changíz's Hulágú, the warlord, gathered no fruit from all his conquests. And Tamerlane, out of all his triumphs, reaped only the peoples blown to the winds, and universal ruin. And Alexander had nothing to show for his vast victories, except that his son toppled from the throne and Philip and Ptolemy took over the dominions he once had ruled. And what did the first Napoleon gain from subjugating the kings of Europe, except the destruction of flourishing countries, the downfall of their inhabitants, the spreading of terror and anguish across Europe and, at the end of his days, his own captivity? So much for the conquerors and the monuments they leave behind them.

Contrast with this the praiseworthy qualities and the greatness and nobility of Anúshírván the Generous and the Just.[39] That fair-minded monarch came to power at a time when the once solidly established throne of Persia was about to crumble away. With his Divine gift of intellect, he laid the foundations of justice, uprooting oppression and tyranny and gathering the scattered peoples of Persia under the wings of his dominion. Thanks to the restoring influence of his continual care, Persia that had lain withered and desolate was quick-

[39] Sásáníyán king who reigned 531–578 A.D.

ened into life and rapidly changed into the fairest of all flourishing nations. He rebuilt and reinforced the disorganized powers of the state, and the renown of his righteousness and justice echoed across the seven climes,[39a] until the peoples rose up out of their degradation and misery to the heights of felicity and honor. Although he was a Magian, Muḥammad, that Center of creation and Sun of prophethood, said of him: "I was born in the time of a just king," and rejoiced at having come into the world during his reign. Did this illustrious personage achieve his exalted station by virtue of his admirable qualities or rather by reaching out to conquer the earth and spill the blood of its peoples? Observe that he attained to such a distinguished rank in the heart of the world that his greatness still rings out through all the impermanence of time, and he won eternal life. Should We comment on the continuing life of the great, this brief essay would be unduly prolonged, and since it is by no means certain that public opinion in Persia will be materially affected by its perusal, We shall abridge the work, and go on to other matters which come within the purview of the public mind. If, however, it develops that this abridgement produces favorable results, We shall, God willing, write a number of books dealing at length and usefully with fundamental principles of the Divine wisdom in its relation to the phenomenal world.

[39a] i.e., the whole world.

No power on earth can prevail against the armies of justice, and every citadel must fall before them; for men willingly go down under the triumphant strokes of this decisive blade, and desolate places bloom and flourish under the tramplings of this host. There are two mighty banners which, when they cast their shadow across the crown of any king, will cause the influence of his government quickly and easily to penetrate the whole earth, even as if it were the light of the sun: the first of these two banners is wisdom; the second is justice. Against these two most potent forces, the iron hills cannot prevail, and Alexander's wall will break before them. It is clear that life in this fast-fading world is as fleeting and inconstant as the morning wind, and this being so, how fortunate are the great who leave a good name behind them, and the memory of a lifetime spent in the pathway of the good pleasure of God.

> *It is all one, if it be a throne*
> *Or the bare ground under the open sky,*
> *Where the pure soul lays him*
> *Down to die.*[39b]

A conquest can be a praiseworthy thing, and there are times when war becomes the powerful basis of

[39b] Sa'dí, The *Gulistán*, On the Conduct of Kings.

peace, and ruin the very means of reconstruction. If, for example, a high-minded sovereign marshals his troops to block the onset of the insurgent and the aggressor, or again, if he takes the field and distinguishes himself in a struggle to unify a divided state and people, if, in brief, he is waging war for a righteous purpose, then this seeming wrath is mercy itself, and this apparent tyranny the very substance of justice and this warfare the cornerstone of peace. Today, the task befitting great rulers is to establish universal peace, for in this lies the freedom of all peoples.

The fourth phrase of the aforementioned Utterance which points out the way of salvation is: "obedient to the commandments of his Lord." It is certain that man's highest distinction is to be lowly before and obedient to his God; that his greatest glory, his most exalted rank and honor, depend on his close observance of the Divine commands and prohibitions. Religion is the light of the world, and the progress, achievement, and happiness of man result from obedience to the laws set down in the holy Books. Briefly, it is demonstrable that in this life, both outwardly and inwardly the mightiest of structures, the most solidly established, the most enduring, standing guard over the world, assuring both the spiritual and the material perfections of mankind, and protecting the happiness and the civilization of society—is religion.

It is true that there are foolish individuals who have never properly examined the fundamentals of the Divine religions, who have taken as their criterion the behavior of a few religious hypocrites and measured all religious persons by that yardstick, and have on this account concluded that religions are an obstacle to progress, a divisive factor and a cause of malevolence and enmity among peoples. They have not even observed this much, that the principles of the Divine religions can hardly be evaluated by the acts of those who only claim to follow them. For every excellent thing, peerless though it may be, can still be diverted to the wrong ends. A lighted lamp in the hands of an ignorant child or of the blind will not dispel the surrounding darkness nor light up the house—it will set both the bearer and the house on fire. Can we, in such an instance, blame the lamp? No, by the Lord God! To the seeing, a lamp is a guide and will show him his path; but it is a disaster to the blind.

Among those who have repudiated religious faith was the Frenchman, Voltaire, who wrote a great number of books attacking the religions, works which are no better than children's playthings. This individual, taking as his criterion the omissions and commissions of the Pope, the head of the Roman Catholic religion, and the intrigues and quarrels of the spiritual leaders of

Christendom, opened his mouth and caviled at the Spirit of God (Jesus). In the unsoundness of his reasoning, he failed to grasp the true significance of the sacred Scriptures, took exception to certain portions of the revealed Texts and dwelt on the difficulties involved. "And We send down of the Qur'án that which is a healing and a mercy to the faithful: But it shall only add to the ruin of the wicked." [40]

> *The Sage of <u>Gh</u>azna* [41] *told the mystic story*
> *To his veiled hearers, in an allegory:*
> *If those who err see naught in the Qur'án*
> *But only words, it's not to wonder on;*
> *Of all the sun's fire, lighting up the sky*
> *Only the warmth can reach a blind man's eye.* [42]

"Many will He mislead by such parables and many guide: but none will He mislead thereby except the wicked . . ." [43]

It is certain that the greatest of instrumentalities for achieving the advancement and the glory of man, the supreme agency for the enlightenment and the redemption of the world, is love and fellowship and unity among all the members of the human race. Nothing can be effected in the world, not even conceivably, without unity and agreement, and the perfect means for engendering fellowship and union is true religion.

[40] Qur'án 17:84.
[41] The poet Saná'í.
[42] Rúmí, The *Ma<u>th</u>naví*, III, 4229-4231.
[43] Qur'án 2:24.

"Hadst Thou spent all the riches of the earth, Thou couldst not have united their hearts; but God hath united them . . ." [44]

With the advent of the Prophets of God, their power of creating a real union, one which is both external and of the heart, draws together malevolent peoples who have been thirsting for one another's blood, into the one shelter of the Word of God. Then a hundred thousand souls become as one soul, and unnumbered individuals emerge as one body.

> *Once they were as the waves of the sea*
> *That the wind made many out of one.*
> *Then God shed down on them His sun,*
> *And His sun but one can never be.*
> *Souls of dogs and wolves go separately,*
> *But the soul of the lions of God is one.* [45]

The events that transpired at the advent of the Prophets of the past, and Their ways and works and circumstances, are not adequately set down in authoritative histories, and are referred to only in condensed form in the verses of the Qur'án, the Holy Traditions and the Torah. Since, however, all events from the days of Moses until the present time are contained in

[44] Qur'án 8:64.

[45] See Rúmí, The *Mathnaví*, II, 185 and 189. Also the Ḥadíth: "God created the creatures in darkness, then He sprinkled some of His Light upon them. Those whom some of that Light reached took the right way, while those whom it missed wandered from the straight road." Cf. R. A. Nicholson's "The Mathnawí of Jalálu'ddín Rúmí" in the E. J. W. Gibb Memorial Series.

the mighty Qur'án, the authoritative Traditions, the Torah and other reliable sources, We shall content Ourself with brief references here, the purpose being to determine conclusively whether religion is the very basis and root-principle of culture and civilization, or whether as Voltaire and his like suppose, it defeats all social progress, well-being and peace.

To preclude once and for all objections on the part of any of the world's peoples, We shall conduct Our discussion conformably to those authoritative accounts which all nations are agreed upon.

At a time when the Israelites had multiplied in Egypt and were spread throughout the whole country, the Coptic Pharaohs of Egypt determined to strengthen and favor their own Coptic peoples and to degrade and dishonor the children of Israel, whom they regarded as foreigners. Over a long period, the Israelites, divided and scattered, were captive in the hands of the tyrannical Copts, and were scorned and despised by all, so that the meanest of the Copts would freely persecute and lord it over the noblest of the Israelites. The enslavement, wretchedness and helplessness of the Hebrews reached such a pitch that they were never, day or night, secure in their own persons nor able to provide any defense for their wives and families against the tyranny of their Pharaohic captors. Then their food was the fragments of their own broken hearts, and their drink a river of tears. They continued on in this anguish until suddenly Moses, the All-Beauteous, beheld the

Divine Light streaming out of the blessed Vale, the place that was holy ground, and heard the quickening voice of God as it spoke from the flame of that Tree "neither of the East nor of the West," [46] and He stood up in the full panoply of His universal prophethood. In the midst of the Israelites, He blazed out like a lamp of Divine guidance, and by the light of salvation He led that lost people out of the shadows of ignorance into knowledge and perfection. He gathered Israel's scattered tribes into the shelter of the unifying and universal Word of God, and over the heights of union He raised up the banner of harmony, so that within a brief interval those benighted souls became spiritually educated, and they who had been strangers to the truth, rallied to the cause of the oneness of God, and were delivered out of their wretchedness, their indigence, their incomprehension and captivity and achieved a supreme degree of happiness and honor. They emigrated from Egypt, set out for Israel's original homeland, and came to Canaan and Philistia. They first conquered the shores of the River Jordan, and Jericho, and settled in that area, and ultimately all the neighboring regions, such as Phoenicia, Edom and Ammon, came under their sway. In Joshua's time there were thirty-one governments in the hands of the Israelites, and in every noble human attribute—learning, stability, determination, courage, honor, generosity—this people came to surpass all the nations of the earth. When in

[46] Qur'án 24:35.

those days an Israelite would enter a gathering, he was immediately singled out for his many virtues, and even foreign peoples wishing to praise a man would say that he was like an Israelite.

It is furthermore a matter of record in numerous historical works that the philosophers of Greece such as Pythagoras, acquired the major part of their philosophy, both divine and material, from the disciples of Solomon. And Socrates after having eagerly journeyed to meet with some of Israel's most illustrious scholars and divines, on his return to Greece established the concept of the oneness of God and the continuing life of the human soul after it has put off its elemental dust. Ultimately, the ignorant among the Greeks denounced this man who had fathomed the inmost mysteries of wisdom, and rose up to take his life; and then the populace forced the hand of their ruler, and in council assembled they caused Socrates to drink from the poisoned cup.

After the Israelites had advanced along every level of civilization, and had achieved success in the highest possible degree, they began little by little to forget the root-principles of the Mosaic Law and Faith, to busy themselves with rites and ceremonials and to show forth unbecoming conduct. In the days of Rehoboam, the son of Solomon, terrible dissension broke out among them; one of their number, Jeroboam, plotted to get the throne, and it was he who introduced the worship of idols. The strife between Rehoboam and Jeroboam led to centuries of warfare between their descendants, with the result that the tribes of Israel were scattered and disrupted. In brief, it was because they forgot the meaning of the Law of God that they became involved in ignorant fanaticism and blameworthy practices such as insurgence and sedition. Their divines, having concluded that all those essential qualifications of humankind set forth in the Holy Book were by then a dead letter, began to think only of furthering their own selfish interests, and afflicted the people by allowing them to sink into the lowest depths of heedlessness and ignorance. And the fruit of their wrong doing was this, that the old-time glory which had endured so long now changed to degradation, and the rulers of Persia, of Greece, and of Rome, took them over. The banners of their sovereignty were reversed; the ignorance, foolishness, abasement and self-love of their religious leaders and their scholars were brought to light in the coming of Nebuchadnezzar, King of Babylon, who destroyed them. After a general massacre, and the sacking and razing of their houses and even the uprooting of their trees, he took captive whatever remnants his sword had spared and carried them off to Babylon. Seventy years later the descendants of these captives were released and went back to Jerusalem. Then Hezekiah and Ezra reestablished in their midst the fundamental principles of the Holy Book, and day by day the Israelites advanced, and the morning-brightness of their earlier ages dawned again. In a short time, however, great dissensions as to belief and conduct broke out anew, and again the one concern of the Jewish doctors became the promotion of their own selfish purposes, and the reforms that had obtained in Ezra's time were changed to perversity and corruption. The situation worsened to such a degree that time and again, the armies of the republic of Rome and of its rulers conquered Israelite territory. Finally the warlike Titus, commander of the Roman forces, trampled the Jewish homeland into dust, putting every man to the sword, taking the women and children captive, flattening their houses, tearing out their trees, burning their books, looting their treasures, and reducing Jerusalem and the Temple to an ash heap. After this supreme calamity, the star of Israel's dominion sank away to nothing, and to this day, the remnant of that vanished nation has been scattered to the four winds. "Humiliation and misery were stamped upon them." [47] These two most great afflictions, brought on by Nebuchadnezzar and Titus, are referred to in the glorious Qur'án: "And We solemnly declared to the children of Israel in the Book, 'Twice surely will ye commit evil in the earth, and with great loftiness of pride will ye surely be uplifted.' And when the menace for the first of the two came to be executed, We sent against you Our servants endowed with terrible prowess; and they searched the inmost part of your abodes, and the menace was accomplished . . . And when the punishment threatened for your latter

[47] Qur'án 2:58.

transgression came to be inflicted, then We sent an enemy to sadden your faces, and to enter the Temple as they entered it at first, and to destroy with utter destruction that which they had conquered." [48]

Our purpose is to show how true religion promotes the civilization and honor, the prosperity and prestige, the learning and advancement of a people once abject, enslaved and ignorant, and how, when it falls into the hands of religious leaders who are foolish and fanatical, it is diverted to the wrong ends, until this greatest of splendors turns into blackest night.

When for the second time the unmistakable signs of Israel's disintegration, abasement, subjection and annihilation had become apparent, then the sweet and holy breathings of the Spirit of God (Jesus) were shed across Jordan and the land of Galilee; the cloud of Divine pity overspread those skies, and rained down the copious waters of the spirit, and after those swelling showers that came from the most great Sea, the Holy Land put forth its perfume and blossomed with the knowledge of God. Then the solemn Gospel song rose up till it rang in the ears of those who dwell in the chambers of heaven, and at the touch of Jesus' breath the unmindful dead that lay in the graves of their ignorance lifted up their heads to receive eternal life. For the space of three years, that Luminary of perfections walked about the fields of Palestine and in the neighborhood of Jerusalem, leading all men into the dawn

[48] Qur'án 17:4 ff.

of redemption, teaching them how to acquire spiritual qualities and attributes well-pleasing to God. Had the people of Israel believed in that beauteous Countenance, they would have girded themselves to serve and obey Him heart and soul, and through the quickening fragrance of His Spirit they would have regained their lost vitality and gone on to new victories.

Alas, of what avail was it; they turned away and opposed Him. They rose up and tormented that Source of Divine knowledge, that Point where the Revelation had come down—all except for a handful who, turning their faces toward God, were cleansed of the stain of this world and found their way to the heights of the placeless Realm. They inflicted every agony on that Wellspring of grace until it became impossible for Him to live in the towns, and still He lifted up the flag of salvation and solidly established the fundamentals of human righteousness, that essential basis of true civilization.

In the fifth chapter of Matthew beginning with the thirty-seventh verse He counsels: "Resist not evil and injury with its like; but whosoever shall smite thee on thy right cheek, turn to him the other also." And further, from the forty-third verse: "Ye have heard that it hath been said, 'Thou shalt love thy neighbor, and thou shalt not vex thine enemy with enmity.' [49] But I

[49] The King James Bible reads: "Ye have heard that it hath been said, Thou shalt love thy neighbour, and hate thine enemy." Scholars object to this reading because it is contrary to the known

81

say unto you, love your enemies, bless them that curse you, do good to them that hate you, and pray for them which despitefully use you, and persecute you; that ye may be the children of your Father which is in heaven: for He maketh His sun to rise on the evil and on the good, and sendeth down the rain of His mercy on the just and on the unjust. For if ye love them which love you, what reward have ye? Do not even the publicans the same?"

Many were the counsels of this kind that were uttered by that Dayspring of Divine wisdom, and souls who have become characterized with such attributes of holiness are the distilled essence of creation and the sources of true civilization

Jesus, then, founded the sacred Law on a basis of moral character and complete spirituality, and for those who believed in Him He delineated a special way of life which constitutes the highest type of action on earth. And while those emblems of redemption were to outward seeming abandoned to the malevolence and persecution of their tormentors, in reality they had been delivered out of the hopeless darkness which encompassed the Jews and they shone forth in everlasting glory at the dawn of that new day.

That mighty Jewish nation toppled and crumbled away, but those few souls who sought shelter beneath

---

Law as set forth in Leviticus 19:18, Exodus 23:4-5, Proverbs 25:21, the Talmud, etc.

the Messianic Tree transformed all human life. At that time the peoples of the world were utterly ignorant, fanatical and idolatrous. Only a small group of Jews professed belief in the oneness of God and they were wretched outcasts. These holy Christian souls now stood up to promulgate a Cause which was diametrically opposed and repugnant to the beliefs of the entire human race. The kings of four out of the world's five continents inexorably resolved to wipe out the followers of Christ, and nevertheless in the end most of them set about promoting the Faith of God with their whole hearts; all the nations of Europe, many of the peoples of Asia and Africa, and some of the inhabitants of the islands of the Pacific, were gathered into the shelter of the oneness of God.

Consider whether there exists anywhere in creation a principle mightier in every sense than religion, or whether any conceivable power is more pervasive than the various Divine Faiths, or whether any agency can bring about real love and fellowship and union among all peoples as can belief in an almighty and all-knowing God, or whether except for the laws of God there has been any evidence of an instrumentality for educating all mankind in every phase of righteousness.

Those qualities which the philosophers attained when they had reached the very heights of their wisdom, those noble human attributes which characterized them at the peak of their perfection, would be exemplified by the believers as soon as they accepted the

Faith. Observe how those souls who drank the living waters of redemption at the gracious hands of Jesus, the Spirit of God, and came into the sheltering shade of the Gospel, attained to such a high plane of moral conduct that Galen, the celebrated physician, although not himself a Christian, in his summary of Plato's *Republic* extolled their actions. A literal translation of his words is as follows:

"The generality of mankind are unable to grasp a sequence of logical arguments. For this reason they stand in need of symbols and parables telling of rewards and punishments in the next world. A confirmatory evidence of this is that today we observe a people called Christians, who believe devoutly in rewards and punishments in a future state. This group show forth excellent actions, similar to the actions of an individual who is a true philosopher. For example, we all see with our own eyes that they have no fear of death, and their passion for justice and fair-dealing is so great that they should be considered true philosophers." [50]

The station of a philosopher, in that age and in the mind of Galen, was superior to any other station in the world. Consider then how the enlightening and spiritualizing power of divine religions impels the believers to such heights of perfection that a philosopher like

[50] Cf. 'Abdu'l-Bahá, *Some Answered Questions*, ch. LXXXIV, and *Promulgation of Universal Peace*, p. 385. See also *Galen on Jews and Christians* by Richard Walzer, Oxford University Press, 1949, p. 15. The author states that Galen's summary here referred to is lost, being preserved only in Arabic quotations.

Galen, not himself a Christian, offers such testimony.

One demonstration of the excellent character of the Christians in those days was their dedication to charity and good works, and the fact that they founded hospitals and philanthropic institutions. For example, the first person to establish public clinics throughout the Roman Empire where the poor, the injured and the helpless received medical care, was the Emperor Constantine. This great king was the first Roman ruler to champion the Cause of Christ. He spared no efforts, dedicating his life to the promotion of the principles of the Gospel, and he solidly established the Roman government, which in reality had been nothing but a system of unrelieved oppression, on moderation and justice. His blessed name shines out across the dawn of history like the morning star, and his rank and fame among the world's noblest and most highly civilized is still on the tongues of Christians of all denominations.

What a firm foundation of excellent character was laid down in those days, thanks to the training of holy souls who arose to promote the teachings of the Gospel. How many primary schools, colleges, hospitals, were established, and institutions where fatherless and indigent children received their education. How many were the individuals who sacrificed their own personal advantages and "out of desire to please the Lord" [51] devoted the days of their lives to teaching the masses.

When, however, the time approached for the efful-

[51] From Qur'án 4:114; 2:207, etc.

85

gent beauty of Muḥammad to dawn upon the world, the control of Christian affairs passed into the hands of ignorant priests. Those heavenly breezes, soft-flowing from the regions of Divine grace, died away, and the laws of the great Evangel, the rock-foundation on which the civilization of the world was based, turned barren of results, this out of misuse and because of the conduct of persons who, seemingly fair, were yet inwardly foul.

The noted historians of Europe, in describing the conditions, manners, politics, learning and culture, in all their aspects, of early, medieval and modern times, unanimously record that during the ten centuries constituting the Middle Ages, from the beginning of the sixth century of the Christian era till the close of the fifteenth, Europe was in every respect and to an extreme degree, barbaric and dark. The principal cause of this was that the monks, referred to by European peoples as spiritual and religious leaders, had given up the abiding glory that comes from obedience to the sacred commandments and heavenly teachings of the Gospel, and had joined forces with the presumptuous and tyrannical rulers of the temporal governments of those times. They had turned their eyes away from everlasting glory, and were devoting all their efforts to the furtherance of their mutual worldly interests and passing and perishable advantages. Ultimately things reached a point where the masses were hopeless prisoners in the hands of these two groups, and all this brought down in ruins the whole structure of the religion, culture, welfare and civilization of the peoples of Europe.

When the unworthy acts and thoughts and the discreditable purposes of the leaders had stilled the sweet savors of the Spirit of God (Jesus) and they ceased to stream across the world, and the darkness of ignorance and bigotry and of actions that were displeasing to God, encompassed the earth, then the dawn of hope shone out and the Divine spring drew on; a cloud of mercy overspread the world, and out of the regions of grace the fecund winds began to blow. In the sign of Muḥammad, the Sun of Truth rose over Yathrib (Medina) and the Ḥijáz and cast across the universe the lights of eternal glory. Then the earth of human potentialities was transformed, and the words "The earth shall shine with the light of her Lord," [52] were fulfilled. The old world turned new again, and its dead body rose into abundant life. Then tyranny and ignorance were overthrown, and towering palaces of knowledge and justice were reared in their place. A sea of enlightenment thundered, and science cast down its rays. The savage peoples of the Ḥijáz, before that Flame of supreme Prophethood was lit in the lamp of Mecca, were the most brutish and benighted of all the peoples of the earth. In all the histories, their depraved and vicious practices, their ferocity and their constant feuds, are a matter of record. In those days the civilized peoples of

[52] Qur'án 39:69.

the world did not even consider the Arab tribes of Mecca and Medina as human beings. And yet, after the Light of the World rose over them, they were—because of the education bestowed on them by that Mine of perfections, that Focal Center of Revelation, and the blessings vouchsafed by the Divine Law—within a brief interval gathered into the shelter of the principle of Divine oneness. This brutish people then attained such a high degree of human perfection and civilization that all their contemporaries marveled at them. Those very peoples who had always mocked the Arabs and held them up to ridicule as a breed devoid of judgment, now eagerly sought them out, visiting their countries to acquire enlightenment and culture, technical skills, statecraft, arts and sciences.

Observe the influence on material situations of that training which is inculcated by the true Educator. Here were tribes so benighted and untamed that during the period of the Jáhilíyyih they would bury their seven-year-old daughters alive—an act which even an animal, let alone a human being, would hate and shrink from but which they in their extreme degradation considered the ultimate expression of honor and devotion to principle—and this darkened people, thanks to the manifest teachings of that great Personage, advanced to such a degree that after they conquered Egypt, Syria and its capital Damascus, Chaldea, Mesopotamia and Írán, they came to administer single-handedly whatever matters were of major importance in four main regions of the globe.

The Arabs then excelled all the peoples of the world in science and the arts, in industry and invention, in philosophy, government and moral character. And truly, the rise of this brutish and despicable element, in such a short interval, to the supreme heights of human perfection, is the greatest demonstration of the rightfulness of the Lord Muḥammad's Prophethood.

In the early ages of Islám the peoples of Europe acquired the sciences and arts of civilization from Islám as practiced by the inhabitants of Andalusia. A careful and thorough investigation of the historical record will establish the fact that the major part of the civilization of Europe is derived from Islám; for all the writings of Muslim scholars and divines and philosophers were gradually collected in Europe and were with the most painstaking care weighed and debated at academic gatherings and in the centers of learning, after which their valued contents would be put to use. Today, numerous copies of the works of Muslim scholars which are not to be found in Islamic countries, are available in the libraries of Europe. Furthermore, the laws and principles current in all European countries are derived to a considerable degree and indeed virtually in their entirety from the works on jurisprudence and the legal decision of Muslim theologians. Were it not for the fear of unduly lengthening the present text, We would cite these borrowings one by one.

The beginnings of European civilization date from the seventh century of the Muslim era. The particulars were these: toward the end of the fifth century of the hegira, the Pope or Head of Christendom set up a great hue and cry over the fact that places sacred to the Christians, such as Jerusalem, Bethlehem and Nazareth, had fallen under Muslim rule, and he stirred up the kings and the commoners of Europe to undertake what he considered a holy war. His impassioned outcry waxed so loud that all the countries of Europe responded, and crusading kings at the head of innumerable hosts passed over the Sea of Marmara and made their way to the continent of Asia. In those days the Fátimid caliphs ruled over Egypt and some countries of the West, and most of the time the kings of Syria, that is the Saljúqs, were subject to them as well. Briefly, the kings of the West with their unnumbered armies fell upon Syria and Egypt, and there was continuous warfare between the Syrian rulers and those of Europe for a period of two hundred and three years. Reinforcements were always coming in from Europe, and time and time again the Western rulers stormed and took over every castle in Syria, and as often, the kings of Islám delivered them out of their hands. Finally Saladin, in the year 693 A.H., drove the European kings and their armies out of Egypt and off the Syrian coast. Hopelessly beaten, they went back to Europe. In the course of these wars of the Crusades, millions of human beings perished. To sum up, from 490 A.H. until

693, kings, commanders and other European leaders continually came and went between Egypt, Syria and the West, and when in the end they all returned home, they introduced into Europe whatever they had observed over two hundred and odd years in Muslim countries as to government, social development and learning, colleges, schools and the refinements of living. The civilization of Europe dates from that time.

O people of Persia! How long will your torpor and lethargy last? You were once the lords of the whole earth; the world was at your beck and call. How is it that your glory has lapsed and you have fallen from favor now, and crept away into some corner of oblivion? You were the fountainhead of learning, the unfailing spring of light for all the earth, how is it that you are withered now, and quenched, and faint of heart? You who once lit the world, how is it that you lurk, inert, bemused, in darkness now? Open your mind's eye, see your great and present need. Rise up and struggle, seek education, seek enlightenment. Is it meet that a foreign people should receive from your own forbears its culture and its knowledge, and that you, their blood, their rightful heirs, should go without? How does it seem, when your neighbors are at work by day and night with their whole hearts, providing for their advancement, their honor and prosperity, that you, in your ignorant fanaticism, are busy only with your quarrels and antipathies, your indulgences and appetites and empty dreams? Is it commendable that you should waste and fritter away in apathy the brilliance that is your birthright, your native competence, your inborn understanding? Again, We have digressed from Our theme.

Those European intellectuals who are well-informed as to the facts of Europe's past, and are characterized by truthfulness and a sense of justice, unanimously acknowledge that in every particular the basic elements of their civilization are derived from Islám. For example Draper,[53] the well-

[53] The Persian text transliterates this author's name as "Draybár" and titles his work The Progress of Peoples. The reference is apparently to John William Draper, 1811–1882, celebrated chemist and widely-translated historian. Detailed material on Muslim contributions to the West, and on Gerbert (Pope Sylvester II) appears in the second volume of the work cited. Of some of Europe's systematically unacknowledged obligations to Islám the author writes: "Injustice founded on religious rancour and national conceit cannot be perpetuated for ever." (Vol. II, p. 42, Rev. ed.) The Dictionary of American Biography states that Draper's father was a Roman Catholic who assumed the name John Christopher Draper when disowned by his family for be-

known French authority, a writer whose accuracy, ability and learning are attested by all European scholars, in one of his best-known works, *The Intellectual Development of Europe,* has written a detailed account in this connection, that is, with reference to the derivation by the peoples of Europe of the fundamentals of civilization and the bases of progress and well-being from Islám. His account is exhaustive, and a translation here would unduly lengthen out the present work and would indeed be irrelevant to Our purpose. If further details are desired the reader may refer to that text.

In essence, the author shows how the totality of Europe's civilization—its laws, principles, institutions, its sciences, philosophies, varied learning, its civilized manners and customs, its literature, art and industry, its organization, its discipline, its behavior, its commendable character traits, and even many of the words

coming a Methodist, and that his real name is unknown. The translator is indebted to Mr. Paul North Rice, Chief of the New York Public Library's Reference Department, for the information that available data on Draper's family history and nationality are in conflict; *The Drapers in America* by Thomas Waln-Morgan (1892) states that Draper's father was born in London, while Albert E. Henschel in "Centenary of John William Draper" (New York University "Colonnade," June, 1911) has the following: "If there be among us any who trace their lineage to the sunny fields of Italy, they may feel a just pride in John William Draper, for his father, John C. Draper, was an Italian by birth . . ."

The translator's thanks are also due to Madame Laura Dreyfus-Barney for investigations in connection with this passage at the Library of Congress and the Bibliothéque Nationale.

current in the French language, derives from the Arabs. One by one, he investigates each of these elements in detail, even giving the period when each was brought over from Islám. He describes as well the arrival of the Arabs in the West, in what is now Spain, and how in a short time they established a well-developed civilization there, and to what a high degree of excellence their administrative system and scholarship attained, and how solidly founded and well regulated were their schools and colleges, where sciences and philosophy, arts and crafts, were taught; what a high level of leadership they achieved in the arts of civilization and how many were the children of Europe's leading families who were sent to attend the schools of Cordova and Granada, Seville and Toledo to acquire the sciences and arts of civilized life. He even records that a European named Gerbert came to the West and enrolled at the University of Cordova in Arab territory, studied arts and sciences there, and after his return to Europe achieved such prominence that ultimately he was elevated to the leadership of the Catholic Church and became the Pope.

The purpose of these references is to establish the fact that the religions of God are the true source of the spiritual and material perfections of man, and the fountainhead for all mankind of enlightenment and beneficial knowledge. If one observes the matter justly it will be found that all the laws of politics are contained in these few and holy words:

"And they enjoin what is just, and forbid what is unjust, and speed on in good works. These are of the righteous." [54] And again: "that there may be among you a people who invite to the good, and enjoin the just, and forbid the wrong. These are they with whom it shall be well." [55] And further: "Verily, God enjoineth justice and the doing of good . . . and He forbiddeth wickedness and oppression. He warneth you that haply ye may be mindful." [56] And yet again, of the civilizing of human behavior: "Make due allowances; and enjoin what is just, and withdraw from the ignorant." [57] And likewise: ". . . who master their anger, and forgive others! God loveth the doers of good." [58] And again: "There is no righteousness in turning your faces toward the East or the West, but he is righteous who believeth in God, and the last day, and the angels, and the Scriptures, and the Prophets; who for the love of God disburseth his wealth to his kindred, and to orphans, and the needy and the wayfarer, and those who ask, and for ransom; who observeth prayer, and payeth the legal alms, and who is of those who perform their covenant when they have covenanted, and are patient under ills and hardships, and in time of trouble: these are they who are just, and these are they

[54] Qur'án 3:110.
[55] Qur'án 3:100.
[56] Qur'án 16:92.
[57] Qur'án 7:198.
[58] Qur'án 3:128.

who fear the Lord." [59] And yet further: "They prefer them before themselves, though poverty be their own lot." [60] See how these few sacred verses encompass the highest levels and innermost meanings of civilization and embody all the excellencies of human character.

By the Lord God, and there is no God but He, even the minutest details of civilized life derive from the grace of the Prophets of God. What thing of value to mankind has ever come into being which was not first set forth either directly or by implication in the Holy Scriptures?

Alas, of what avail is it. When the weapons are in cowards' hands, no man's life and property are safe, and thieves only grow the stronger. When, in the same way, a far-from-perfect priesthood acquire control of affairs, they come down like a massive curtain between the people and the light of Faith.

Sincerity is the foundation-stone of faith. That is, a religious individual must disregard his personal desires and seek in whatever way he can wholeheartedly to serve the public interest; and it is impossible for a human being to turn aside from his own selfish advantages and sacrifice his own good for the good of the community except through true religious faith. For self-love is kneaded into the very clay of man, and it is not possible that, without any hope of a substantial reward, he should neglect his own present material

[59] Qur'án 2:172.
[60] Qur'án 59:9.

good. That individual, however, who puts his faith in God and believes in the words of God—because he is promised and certain of a plentiful reward in the next life, and because worldly benefits as compared to the abiding joy and glory of future planes of existence are nothing to him—will for the sake of God abandon his own peace and profit and will freely consecrate his heart and soul to the common good. "A man, too, there is who selleth his very self out of desire to please God." [61]

There are some who imagine that an innate sense of human dignity will prevent man from committing evil actions and insure his spiritual and material perfection. That is, that an individual who is characterized with natural intelligence, high resolve, and a driving zeal, will, without any consideration for the severe punishments consequent on evil acts, or for the great rewards of righteousness, instinctively refrain from inflicting harm on his fellow men and will hunger and thirst to do good. And yet, if we ponder the lessons of history it will become evident that this very sense of honor and dignity is itself one of the bounties deriving from the instructions of the Prophets of God. We also observe in infants the signs of aggression and lawlessness, and that if a child is deprived of a teacher's instructions his undesirable qualities increase from one moment to the next. It is therefore clear that the emergence of this natural sense of human dignity and honor is the result

[61] Qur'án 2:203.

of education. Secondly, even if we grant for the sake of the argument that instinctive intelligence and an innate moral quality would prevent wrongdoing, it is obvious that individuals so characterized are as rare as the philosopher's stone. An assumption of this sort cannot be validated by mere words, it must be supported by the facts. Let us see what power in creation impels the masses toward righteous aims and deeds!

Aside from this, if that rare individual who does exemplify such a faculty should also become an embodiment of the fear of God, it is certain that his strivings toward righteousness would be strongly reinforced.

Universal benefits derive from the grace of the Divine religions, for they lead their true followers to sincerity of intent, to high purpose, to purity and spotless honor, to surpassing kindness and compassion, to the keeping of their covenants when they have covenanted, to concern for the rights of others, to liberality, to justice in every aspect of life, to humanity and philanthropy, to valor and to unflagging efforts in the service of mankind. It is religion, to sum up, which produces all human virtues, and it is these virtues which are the bright candles of civilization. If a man is not characterized by these excellent qualities, it is certain that he has never attained to so much as a drop out of the fathomless river of the waters of life that flows through the teachings of the Holy Books, nor caught the faintest breath of the fragrant breezes that blow from the gardens of God; for nothing on earth can be demonstrated by words alone, and every level of existence is known by its signs and symbols, and every degree in man's development has its identifying mark.

The purpose of these statements is to make it abundantly clear that the Divine religions, the holy precepts, the heavenly teachings, are the unassailable basis of human happiness, and that the peoples of the world can hope for no real relief or deliverance without this one great remedy. This panacea must, however, be administered by a wise and skilled physician, for in the hands of an incompetent all the cures that the Lord of men has ever created to heal men's ills could produce no health, and would on the contrary only destroy the helpless and burden the hearts of the already afflicted.

That Source of Divine wisdom, that Manifestation of Universal Prophethood (Muḥammad), encouraging mankind to acquire sciences and arts and similar advantages has commanded them to seek these even in the furthermost reaches of China; yet the incompetent and caviling doctors forbid this, offering as their justification the saying, "He who imitates a people is one of them." They have not even grasped what is meant by the "imitation" referred to, nor do they know that the Divine religions enjoin upon and encourage all the faithful to adopt such principles as will conduce to continuous improvements, and to acquire from other peoples sciences and arts. Whoever expresses himself to the contrary has never drunk of the nectar of knowledge and is astray in his own ignorance, groping after the mirage of his desires.

Judge this aright: which one of these modern developments, whether in themselves or in their application, is contrary to the Divine commandments? If they mean the establishment of parliaments, these are enjoined by the very text of the holy verse: "and whose affairs are guided by mutual counsel." [62] And again, addressing the Dayspring of all knowledge, the Source of perfection (Muḥammad), in spite of His being in possession of universal wisdom, the words are: "and consult them in the affair." [63] In view of this how can the question of mutual consultation be in conflict with the religious Law? The great advantages of consultation can be established by logical arguments as well.

Can they say that it would be contrary to the laws of God to make a death sentence conditional on the most careful investigations, on the sanction of numerous bodies, on legal proof and the royal order? Can they claim that what went on under the previous government was in conformity with the Qur'án? For example, in the days when Ḥájí Mírzá Áqásí was Prime Minister, it was heard from many sources that the governor of Gulpáygán seized thirteen defenseless bailiffs of that region, all of them of holy lineage, all of them guiltless, and without a trial, and without obtaining any higher sanction, beheaded them in a single hour.

[62] Qur'án 42:36.
[63] Qur'án 3:153.

At one time the population of Persia exceeded fifty millions. This has been dissipated partly through civil wars, but predominantly because of the lack of an adequate system of government and the despotism and unbridled authority of provincial and local governors. With the passage of time, not one-fifth of the population has survived, for the governors would select any victim they cared to, however innocent, and vent their wrath on him and destroy him. Or, for a whim, they would make a pet out of some proven mass murderer. Not a soul could speak out, because the governor was in absolute control. Can we say that these things were in conformity with justice or with the laws of God?

Can we maintain that it is contrary to the fundamentals of the Faith to encourage the acquisition of useful arts and of general knowledge, to inform oneself as to the truths of such physical sciences as are beneficial to man, and to widen the scope of industry and increase the products of commerce and multiply the nation's avenues of wealth? Would it conflict with the worship of God to establish law and order in the cities and organize the rural districts, to repair the roads and build railroads and facilitate transportation and travel and thus increase the people's well-being? Would it be inconsistent with the Divine commands and prohibitions if we were to work the abandoned mines which are the greatest source of the nation's wealth, and to build factories, from which come the entire people's comfort, security and affluence? Or to stimulate the creation of new industries and to promote improvements in our domestic products?

By the All-Glorious! I am astonished to find what a veil has fallen across their eyes, and how it blinds them even to such obvious necessities as these. And there is no doubt whatever that when conclusive arguments and proofs of this sort are advanced, they will answer, out of a thousand hidden spites and prejudices: "On the Day of Judgment, when men stand before their Lord, they will not be questioned as to their education and the degree of their culture—rather will they be examined as to their good deeds." Let us grant this and assume that man will not be asked as to his culture and education; even so, on that great Day of Reckoning, will not the leaders be called to account? Will it not be said to them: "O chiefs and leaders! Why did ye cause this mighty nation to fall from the heights of its former glory, to pass from its place at the heart and center of the civilized world? Ye were well able to take hold of such measures as would lead to the high honor of this people. This ye failed to do, and ye even went on to deprive them of the common benefits enjoyed by all. Did not this people once shine out like stars in an auspicious heaven? How have ye dared to quench their light in darkness! Ye could have lit the lamp of temporal and eternal glory for them; why did ye fail to strive for this with all your hearts? And when by God's grace a flaming Light flared up, why did ye fail to shelter it in the glass of your valor, from the winds that beat against it? Why did ye rise up in all your might to put it out?"

"And every man's fate have We fastened about his neck: and on the Day of Resurrection will We bring it forth to him a book which shall be proffered to him wide open." [64]

Again, is there any deed in the world that would be nobler than service to the common good? Is there any greater blessing conceivable for a man, than that he should become the cause of the education, the development, the prosperity and honor of his fellow-creatures? No, by the Lord God! The highest righteousness of all is for blessed souls to take hold of the hands of the helpless and deliver them out of their ignorance and abasement and poverty, and with pure motives, and only for the sake of God, to arise and energetically devote themselves to the service of the masses, forgetting their own worldly advantage and working only to serve the general good. "They prefer them before themselves, though poverty be their own lot." [65] "The best of men are those who serve the people; the worst of men are those who harm the people."

Glory be to God! What an extraordinary situation now obtains, when no one, hearing a claim advanced, asks himself what the speaker's real motive might be, and what selfish purpose he might not have hidden behind the mask of words. You find, for example, that an

[64] Qur'án 17:14.
[65] Qur'án 59:9.

individual seeking to further his own petty and personal concerns, will block the advancement of an entire people. To turn his own water mill, he will let the farms and fields of all the others parch and wither. To maintain his own leadership, he will everlastingly direct the masses toward that prejudice and fanaticism which subvert the very base of civilization.

Such a man, at the same moment that he is perpetrating actions which are anathema in the sight of God and detested by all the Prophets and Holy Ones, if he sees a person who has just finished eating wash his hands with soap—an article the inventor of which was 'Abdu'lláh Búní, a Muslim—will, because this unfortunate does not instead wipe his hands up and down the front of his robe and on his beard, set up a hue and cry to the effect that the religious law has been overthrown, and the manners and customs of heathen nations are being introduced into ours. Utterly disregarding the evil of his own ways, he considers the very cause of cleanliness and refinement as wicked and foolish.

O People of Persia! Open your eyes! Pay heed! Release yourselves from this blind following of the bigots, this senseless imitation which is the principal reason why men fall away into paths of ignorance and degradation. See the true state of things. Rise up; seize hold of such means as will bring you life and happiness and greatness and glory among all the nations of the world.

The winds of the true springtide are passing over

you; adorn yourselves with blossoms like trees in the
scented garden. Spring clouds are streaming; then turn
you fresh and verdant like the sweet eternal fields. The
dawn star is shining, set your feet on the true path. The
sea of might is swelling, hasten to the shores of high
resolve and fortune. The pure water of life is welling
up, why wear away your days in a desert of thirst? Aim
high, choose noble ends; how long this lethargy, how
long this negligence! Despair, both here and hereafter,
is all you will gain from self-indulgence; abomination
and misery are all you will harvest from fanaticism,
from believing the foolish and the mindless. The confirmations of God are supporting you, the succor of
God is at hand: why do you not cry out and exult with
all your heart, and strive with all your soul!

Among those matters which require thorough re-
vision and reform is the method of studying the
various branches of knowledge and the organization of the academic curriculum. From lack of
organization, education has become haphazard and confused. Trifling subjects which should not call for
elaboration receive undue attention, to such an extent
that students, over long periods of time, waste their
minds and their energies on material that is pure sup-

position, in no way susceptible of proof, such study consisting in going deep into statements and concepts which careful examination would establish as not even unlikely, but rather as unalloyed superstition, and representing the investigation of useless conceits and the chasing of absurdities. There can be no doubt that to concern oneself with such illusions, to examine into and lengthily debate such idle propositions, is nothing but a waste of time and a marring of the days of one's life. Not only this, but it also prevents the individual from undertaking the study of those arts and sciences of which society stands in dire need. The individual should, prior to engaging in the study of any subject, ask himself what its uses are and what fruit and result will derive from it. If it is a useful branch of knowledge, that is, if society will gain important benefits from it, then he should certainly pursue it with all his heart. If not, if it consists in empty, profitless debates and in a vain concatenation of imaginings that lead to no result except acrimony, why devote one's life to such useless hairsplittings and disputes.

Because this matter requires further elucidation and a thorough hearing, so that it can be fully established that some of the subjects which today are neglected are extremely valuable, while the nation has no need whatever of various other, superfluous studies, the point will, God willing, be developed in a second volume. Our hope is that a reading of this first volume will produce fundamental changes in the thinking and the behavior of society, for We have undertaken the work with a sincere intent and purely for the sake of God. Although in this world individuals who are able to distinguish between sincere intentions and false words are as rare as the philosopher's stone, yet We fix Our hopes on the measureless bounties of the Lord.

To resume: As for that group who maintains that in effecting these necessary reforms we must proceed with deliberation, exercise patience and gain the objectives one at a time, just what do they mean by this? If by deliberation they are referring to that circumspection which the science of government requires, their thought is timely and appropriate. It is certain that momentous undertakings cannot be brought to a successful conclusion in haste; that in such cases haste would only make waste.

The world of politics is like the world of man; he is seed at first, and then passes by degrees to the condition of embryo and foetus, acquiring a bone structure, being clothed with flesh, taking on his own special form, until at last he reaches the plane where he can befittingly fulfill the words: "the most excellent of Makers." [66] Just as this is a requirement of creation and is based on the universal Wisdom, the political world in the same way cannot instantaneously evolve from the nadir of defectiveness to the zenith of rightness and perfection. Rather, qualified individuals must strive by

[66] Qur'án 23:14: "Blessed therefore be God, the most excellent of Makers."

day and by night, using all those means which will conduce to progress, until the government and the people develop along every line from day to day and even from moment to moment.

When, through the Divine bestowals, three things appear on earth, this world of dust will come alive, and stand forth wondrously adorned and full of grace. These are first, the fruitful winds of spring; second, the welling plenty of spring clouds; and third, the heat of the bright sun. When, out of the endless bounty of God, these three have been vouchsafed, then slowly, by His leave, dry trees and branches turn fresh and green again, and array themselves with many kinds of blossoms and fruits. It is the same when the pure intentions and the justice of the ruler, the wisdom and consummate skill and statecraft of the governing authorities, and the determination and unstinted efforts of the people, are all combined; then day by day the effects of the advancement, of the far-reaching reforms, of the pride and prosperity of government and people alike, will become clearly manifest.

If, however, by delay and postponement they mean this, that in each generation only one minute section of the necessary reforms should be attended to, this is nothing but lethargy and inertia, and no results would be forthcoming from such a procedure, except the endless repetition of idle words. If haste is harmful, inertness and indolence are a thousand times worse. A middle course is best, as it is written: "It is incumbent upon you to do good between the two evils," this referring to the mean between the two extremes. "And let not thy hand be tied up to thy neck; nor yet open it with all openness . . . but between these follow a middle way." [67]

The primary, the most urgent requirement is the promotion of education. It is inconceivable that any nation should achieve prosperity and success unless this paramount, this fundamental concern is carried forward. The principal reason for the decline and fall of peoples is ignorance. Today the mass of the people are uninformed even as to ordinary affairs, how much less do they grasp the core of the important problems and complex needs of the time.

It is therefore urgent that beneficial articles and books be written, clearly and definitely establishing what the present-day requirements of the people are, and what will conduce to the happiness and advancement of society. These should be published and spread throughout the nation, so that at least the leaders among the people should become, to some degree, awakened, and arise to exert themselves along those lines which will lead to their abiding honor. The publication of high thoughts is the dynamic power in the arteries of life; it is the very soul of the world. Thoughts are a boundless sea, and the effects and varying conditions of existence are as the separate forms and individual limits of the waves; not until the sea boils up will the waves

[67] Qur'án 17:31; 110.

rise and scatter their pearls of knowledge on the shore of life.

> *Thou, Brother, art thy thought alone,*
> *The rest is only thew and bone.*[68]

Public opinion must be directed toward whatever is worthy of this day, and this is impossible except through the use of adequate arguments and the adducing of clear, comprehensive and conclusive proofs. For the helpless masses know nothing of the world, and while there is no doubt that they seek and long for their own happiness, yet ignorance like a heavy veil shuts them away from it.

Observe to what a degree the lack of education will weaken and degrade a people. Today [1875] from the standpoint of population the greatest nation in the world is China, which has something over four hundred million inhabitants. On this account, its government should be the most distinguished on earth, its people the most acclaimed. And yet on the contrary, because of its lack of education in cultural and material civilization, it is the feeblest and the most helpless of all weak nations. Not long ago, a small contingent of English and French troops went to war with China and defeated that country so decisively that they took over its capital Peking. Had the Chinese government

---

[68] Rúmí, The *Mathnaví*, II 2:277. The next line is:
A garden close, if that thought be a rose,
But if it be a thorn, then only fit to burn.

and people been abreast of the advanced sciences of the day, had they been skilled in the arts of civilization, then if all the nations on earth had marched against them the attack would still have failed, and the attackers would have returned defeated whence they had come.

Stranger even than this episode is the fact that the government of Japan was in the beginning subject to and under the protection of China, and that now for some years, Japan has opened its eyes and adopted the techniques of contemporary progress and civilization, promoting sciences and industries of use to the public, and striving to the utmost of their power and competence until public opinion was focused on reform. This government has currently advanced to such a point that, although its population is only one-sixth, or even one-tenth, that of China, it has recently challenged the latter government, and China has finally been forced to come to terms. Observe carefully how education and the arts of civilization bring honor, prosperity, independence and freedom to a government and its people.

It is, furthermore, a vital necessity to establish schools throughout Persia, even in the smallest country towns and villages, and to encourage the people in every possible way to have their children learn to read and write. If necessary, education should even be made compulsory. Until the nerves and arteries of the nation stir into life, every measure that is attempted will prove vain; for the people are as the human body, and determination and the will to struggle are as the soul, and a soulless body does not move. This dynamic power is present to a superlative degree in the very nature of the Persian people, and the spread of education will release it.

As to that element who believe that it is neither necessary nor appropriate to borrow the principles of civilization, the fundamentals of progress toward high levels of social happiness in the material world, the laws which effect thorough reforms, the methods which extend the scope of culture—and that it is far more suitable that Persia and the Persians reflect over the situation and then create their own techniques of progress.

It is certain that if the vigorous intelligence and superior skill of the nation's great, and the energy and resolve of the most eminent men at the imperial court, and the determined efforts of those who have knowledge and capacity, and are well versed in the great laws of political life, should all be combined, and all should exert every effort and examine and reflect over every detail as well as on the main currents of affairs, there is every likelihood that because of the effective plans they would evolve, some situations would be thoroughly reformed. In the majority of cases, however, they would still be obliged to borrow; because, throughout the many-centuried past, hundreds of thousands of persons have devoted their entire lives to putting these things to the test until they were able to bring about these substantial developments. If all that is to be ignored and an effort is made to re-create those agencies in our own country and in our own way, and thus effect the hoped-for advancement, many generations would pass by and still the goal would not be reached. Observe for instance that in other countries they persevered over a long period until finally they discovered the power of steam and by means of it were enabled easily to perform the heavy tasks which were once beyond human strength. How many centuries it would take if we were to abandon the use of this power and instead strain every nerve to invent a substitute. It is therefore preferable to keep on with the use of steam and at the same time continuously to examine into the possibility of there being a far greater force available. One should regard the other technological advances, sciences, arts and political formulae of proven usefulness in the same light—i.e., those procedures which, down the ages, have time and again been put to the test and whose many uses and advantages have demonstrably resulted in the glory and greatness of the state, and the well-being and progress of the people. Should all these be abandoned, for no valid reason, and other methods of reform be attempted, by the time such reforms might eventuate, and their advantages might be put to proof, many years would go by, and many lives. Meanwhile, "we are still at the first bend in the road." [69]

The superiority of the present in relation to the past consists in this, that the present can take over and adopt as a model many things which have been tried and tested and the great benefits of which have been demonstrated in the past, and that it can make its own new discoveries and by these augment its valuable inheritance. It is clear, then, that the accomplishment and experience of the past are known and available to the present, while the discoveries peculiar to the present were unknown to the past. This presupposes that the later generation is made up of persons of ability; otherwise, how many a later generation has lacked even so much as a drop out of the boundless ocean of knowledge that was its forbears'.

Reflect a little: let us suppose that, through the power of God, certain individuals are placed on earth; these obviously stand in need of many things, to provide for their human dignity, their happiness and ease. Now is it more practicable for them to acquire these things from their contemporaries, or should they, in each successive generation, borrow nothing, but instead independently create one or another of the instrumentalities which are necessary to human existence?

[69] From the lines: " 'Aṭṭár has passed through the seven cities of love, and we are still at the first bend in the road."

Should some maintain that those laws, principles and fundamentals of progress on the highest levels of a fully developed society, which are current in other countries, are not suited to the condition and the traditional needs of Persia's people, and that on this account it is necessary that within Írán, the nations' planners should exert their utmost efforts to bring about reforms appropriate to Persia—let them first explain what harm could come from such foreign importations.

If the country were built up, the roads repaired, the lot of the helpless improved by various means, the poor rehabilitated, the masses set on the path to progress, the avenues of public wealth increased, the scope of education widened, the government properly organized, and the free exercise of the individual's rights, and the security of his person and property, his dignity and good name, assured—would all this be at odds with the character of the Persian people? Whatever is in conflict with these measures has already been proved injurious, in every country, and does not concern one locality more than another.

These superstitions result in their entirety from lack of wisdom and understanding, and insufficient observation and analysis. Indeed, the majority of the reactionaries and the procrastinators are only concealing their own selfish interests under a barrage of idle words, and confusing the minds of the helpless masses with public statements which bear no relation to their well-concealed objectives.

115

O people of Persia! The heart is a divine trust; cleanse it from the stain of self-love, adorn it with the coronal of pure intent, until the sacred honor, the abiding greatness of this illustrious nation may shine out like the true morning in an auspicious heaven. This handful of days on earth will slip away like shadows and be over. Strive then that God may shed His grace upon you, that you may leave a favorable remembrance in the hearts and on the lips of those to come. "And grant that I be spoken of with honor by posterity." [70]

Happy the soul that shall forget his own good, and like the chosen ones of God, vie with his fellows in service to the good of all; until, strengthened by the blessings and perpetual confirmations of God, he shall be empowered to raise this mighty nation up to its ancient pinnacles of glory, and restore this withered land to sweet new life, and as a spiritual springtime, array those trees which are the lives of men with the fresh leaves, the blossoms and fruits of consecrated joy.

[70] Qur'án 26:84.

INDEX

117

INDEX

Children
Lawless, need education, 97-98
China
Degraded by lack education, 110-111
Rejected of God, idol worship, 26
Christianity
Crusades, 90-91
Middle Ages, worldly, corrupt, 85-87
Propagation by holy deeds, 45
Protestantism growing, 41-46
Story of Nu'mán, 46-51
Christians
Educational institutions founded, 85
Galen praised morals of, 84
People of the Book; Qur'án, 26
Tortured, 45
Transformed world, 82-85
Civilization
Based on: justice, 4, 64-70; power of intellect, 1-3; religion, 72
Destroyed by: fanaticism, prejudice, 104
Education leads to, 103
External, useless, 60
Objective human well-being, 60
Persia could develop perfect, 4
Spiritually learned aid, 33
Virtues of; Qur'án, 95-96
Clergy
Spirituality of not universal, 59
Compassion
Attribute of perfection, 40
Conquest
Praiseworthy at times, 70-71
Conscience
Pray for development of, 2
Constantine, Emperor
Established Roman justice, mercy, 85

Consultation
Bedrock of government, 17
Encouraged by Qur'án, 100
Courage
Attribute of perfection, 40
Courts
Deviation from spiritual law, 18
Written code essential for, 37-38
Creation
Primacy of intellect and wisdom in, 1
Criticism
Harmful to spirituality, 56-57
Crusades
European civilization dates from, 90
Cyrus, King of Persia
Ruler of all ancient world, 7-8

Day of Resurrection
Book wide open; Qur'án, 103
Days of Ignorance
Customs of, retained by Muḥammad, 27-29
Paganism in Arabia, 28-29
Story: Day of Evil, Day of Grace, 46-51
Defender of the Faith
Meaning of, 41
Desire
"Blot out virtue" poem, 64
"Devouring fire" eats up character, 59-60
Devotion
Not relevant to outer appearance, 58
Discipline
Not relevant to outer appearance, 58
Divine Law (*see also* Law)
Purpose in revelation of, 46

118

INDEX

INDEX

INDEX

INDEX

Napoleon I
  Conqueror of three continents, 67
  Futile life, 68
Nation (or state)
  Based on legislative and executive forces, 37
Nations
  Borrow sciences from each other, 32
Nature
  Ignorant, needs education, 97-98
Nebuchadnezzar
  King of Babylon, captured Israelites, 78
Negroes
  African, converted to Protestantism, 42-43
Nu'mán
  Story: Day of Evil, Day of Grace, 46-51

Parliaments
  Elected, increases justice, 23-24
  Must be God-fearing, incorruptible, 17
  Qur'án encourages, 100
Passions
  Oppose, 59-60
Patience
  Under hardships, 95
Peace
  Achievement of, 66
  Covenant, establish, 64-66
  Force cannot bring, 61
  Universal, means to, 64-66, 71
Pentateuch (Torah)
  Laws of Abraham, contains, 29
  Tampered with, 30
People
  Enlightened, 32-36

Perfection
  Attributes of, 35-40
  Nothing to do with appearance, 58-59
  Religion source of, 94-95
Persia
  Ancient civilization, noble, 4
  Army, needs reform, 15-16
  Bigots, cause of degradation, 104
  Books, publications, needed, 109
  Bribery, should be abolished, 15
  Corruption, 8, 15-16
  Culture, education, neglected, 102-6
  Decadence, 8-9, 12
  Foreign relations, recommended, 14-15
  Future depends on education, 4, 116
  Government: despotic, 100-101; first on earth, 8; local, corrupt, 15-16
  History of, learning, power, 6-9
  Ignorance widespread, 3-4, 8
  Justice hampered by ignorance, 18
  Muḥammad borrowed customs from, 27
  Past glory quenched, 91-92
  People of: innate intelligence, 9; ignorant, irreligious, 18
  Population depleted by wars, killing, 101
  Progress: blind to need for, 102; depends on leaders, 112-16
  Public opinion, disunited, 16
  Reforms censured by ignorant, 11-19
  Rich in natural resources, 9-10
  Schools must multiply, 110-12

123

INDEX

124

INDEX

Resurrection (see Day of Resurrection)

Revelation
Influence on civilization, 88

Righteousness
Defined; Qur'án, 95-96
Education of masses, 103
Guidance toward, righteous act, 6
Natural, reinforced by religion, 98

Rome
Conquest of Israelites, 79

Rúmí, Jalálu'ddín
Mathnaví, 34, 73-74, 110

Saladin
Conquered Egypt, Syria, 90

Salvation
Obedience to Lord, 71

Schools
Persia in urgent need of, 109-12

Science
Develops civilizations; not contrary to religion, 101-2
Emanations of mind, 2
Progresses age after age, 113-15
Raises man to excellence, 14
Society stands in dire need, 106

Scientists
Station high, praiseworthy, 21-22

Scriptures
Source of civilization, 96

Selfishness
Contemptible, 4
Criticism of others related to, 56-57

Self-love
Kneaded into man, 96

Servants of God
Oneness of, 39

Service
Common good, noblest, 103
Man's faculties bestowed for, 3

Sháh of Írán (see Persia)

Sin
Blocks progress, 103-4
Indolence, lethargy, 108

Sincerity
Attribute of perfection, 40
Foundation of faith, 96

Socrates
Learned from Israelites, 77

Soap
Invented by a Muslim, 104

Spain
Civil war, 63
Islamic civilization, schools, 94

Spirituality
Aids others, brings progress, 58-59
Foundation of: oppose passions, 59-60
Idleness, condemned, 39-40
Qualities, 33-36, 53-56

Statesmen
Called to account, 102
Rank next to just kings, 20-23

Superstition
Veils from true knowledge, 106

Sword
Reject as means propagate Faith, 43-46

Syria
Ruled by Islám, 90
Saladin captured, 90

Tamerlane
Conqueror of Asia, 67
Futile life, 68

Teaching
Associate with all faiths, 54
Duty every believer, 44
Gentleness, 53

125

INDEX